# TEN
# TO
# ZEN

TEN
MINUTES
A DAY
TO A
CALMER,
HAPPIER
YOU

# TEN
# TO
# ZEN

OWEN O'KANE

CHRONICLE BOOKS
SAN FRANCISCO

First published in the United States in 2019
by Chronicle Books LLC.

First published in the United Kingdom in 2018 by Bluebird,
an imprint of Pan Macmillan.

Library of Congress Cataloging-in-Publication Data available.

ISBN 978-1-4521-8250-6

Printed and bound by CPI Group (UK) Ltd, Croydon, CR0 4YY

10 9 8 7 6 5 4 3 2 1

Chronicle Books LLC
680 Second Street
San Francisco, California 94107

www.chroniclebooks.com

Dedicated to the memory of my mum, Kathleen,
who taught me most about kindness,
compassion, and living life fully.

# CONTENTS

# Introduction

Sometimes life can be hard and situations difficult to manage. In my work as a therapist, I often see people with problems that may be familiar to you:

- Do you ever feel overwhelmed and unable to cope?

- Do you worry constantly and feel exhausted or irritable and angry?

- Have you lost your zest for life and sense of fun?

- Are you experiencing relationship difficulties?

- Do you over- or under-eat, or rely on stimuli, such as alcohol, medication, drugs, shopping, sex, and social media, to cope?

- Do you ever feel helpless or worthless and that you are just not good enough?

This list is not exhaustive and you may have different challenges, but if some, most, or all of these resonate with you, let me assure you that you are not alone. Help is at hand. My Ten to Zen workout will show you how you can learn to manage these difficult emotions and ultimately live life in a calmer, happier, and more authentic way.

Have you ever looked at all the happy images on social media—Facebook, Twitter, Instagram—and had the envious thought that everyone else is having a great time? This can happen even when we know we are seeing only a carefully edited version of reality. Yes, it's great to share the happy stuff, but where are the rest of the pictures? The narratives we share on social media are what we want others to see and believe of us, while we rarely post about the challenges we are all living with.

What a relief it would be if we could all be truthful about who we really are, without apology. If we could only be honest about the glorious, wonderful confusion it is to be human. Within this confusion there are many insights and possibilities for growth, but these will emerge only if we allow ourselves time to stop and reflect. Our culture promotes distorted news, edited stories, and a frenzied pace of activity, and we all do so much "stuff" that we are often burnt out—even our children. So within this book I encourage you to take time out for just ten minutes every day, with the hope that this time will become a central part of your life. I also encourage you to address some of the difficult aspects of your life in a safe, controlled way, helping you move toward a truer version of yourself.

We all struggle at times—I know this to be true both personally and professionally. This book offers the Ten to Zen solution, a starting point for regaining control and making your way back to a calmer mind and better life. I don't promise to wave a magic wand or sprinkle fairy dust. However, I do promise to share with you some effective, life-changing techniques. These techniques and principles for living are based on some of the best-evidenced psychology models used in my work as a psychotherapist, my experiences of working with the dying, and some of my own personal experiences along the way.

## A Workout with a Difference

My workout stands out from the others partly because of the timing. The beauty of Ten to Zen is that you really do need only ten minutes a day to benefit from it. But it is also different because it goes much more deeply into why we are becoming distressed in the first place.

We all know it is impossible to feel calm and in control all the time, yet finding a way of regaining a sense of perspective is, at times, essential. That doesn't mean it's easy though, and in the initial stages of developing Ten to Zen I thought hard about what an effective daily mind workout might look like. In essence, I wanted it to do the following things:

- To help people find a way of stopping, and slowing down quickly

- To help get them out of their distressed head space

- To help them regain a sense of perspective

- To help them move forward with a greater sense of calm and control

But how would I do this? Initially I knew I would use the techniques I'd picked up from my training in psychological therapies, but I also wanted my approach to be more than a set of skills—I wanted the Ten to Zen workout to embody principles for more peaceful, authentic living. This prompted me to engage with the insights I had gained from my work with both the dying and the living over the past twenty-five years.

So now I ask you to keep an open mind and commit to the time required to practice wholeheartedly. Be prepared for a fresh start, and hold on to the thought that whatever has happened before, that moment has now gone. The only important time is now.

There is space in the "Take a Moment . . ." exercises in this book to write your own notes, or you may prefer to have a special notebook that you use when doing your Ten to Zen workout.

## Influences from the Dying

For many years before becoming a therapist I worked as a nurse in the palliative care world, and I would often hear dying patients talking about regret, and how they wished they had used their time differently. I'm now a senior psychotherapist and, at the time of writing this, a clinical lead working in the National Health Service in the United Kingdom.

I can still hear the voice of a man in his seventies who was in hospice, saying, "I spent so much time worrying during my life, I wish I had learned not to do that."

In fact I have lost count of the number of times I've heard people talk about how stressful life was for them, how they had gotten their priorities wrong and the oh-so-familiar words, "If only I had my time again."

What I learned from these patients is that they felt so much of their precious time had been spent on stuff that wasn't really important. Hearing this sparked my initial desire to develop something to counteract this. I wanted to share with a wider audience what I saw as the privileged experiences I'd had while working as a nurse.

At the same time, I realized that very few people were taking time out of their busy lives to look after their minds. Starting a book by saying that it has partly been influenced by experiences with the dying might seem an odd choice, and some of you might be concerned that the content will be bleak. Let me assure you nothing could be further from the truth; it is life-affirming.

In essence, Ten to Zen is a daily mental workout aimed to help you live life more fully, more deeply, and with more enjoyment. Through my experience working in the world of physical and mental healthcare I have seen that the process of death brings with it many lessons for those who journey alongside—lessons of hope, courage, perspective, and joy, as well as ways to live peacefully with what time we have left.

The numerous insights I've received from the dying could fill a whole other book, and the stories are varied and diverse, but the themes that dominated were often remarkably similar: worry, psychological distress and fear often stopped people from living life as fully and happily and authentically as they would wish.

Being a palliative care nurse brought me face-to-face with people's lives: their happy memories, their priorities, their regrets. I found that they all wished that they'd spent less time stressing about things, that they'd enjoyed the good times more fully, that they'd paid more attention to all the potential pleasures in life. This triggered a desire in me to create an effective, reliable process that everyone can use on a daily basis to calm their minds and to start to live in the here and now. Because in my experience, very few things are as important.

My years as a nurse also motivated me to train profession-ally as a therapist. I could see that the suffering of dying patients was often more than just physical pain and that there was often an underlying psychological aspect to their distress, too. I would sometimes witness that pain being eased when patients were able to unburden their minds in a way they hadn't previously been able. So I also wanted to create some-thing that would help people live in ways that could soothe this psychological distress. What better teachers do we have than those who are facing death? With immense gratitude to those who courageously shared their stories with me, I pass on some of the lessons I learned to you.

So this is how Ten to Zen came to be: a simple, struc-tured workout for the mind that takes just ten minutes out of your day yet will have far-reaching, truly life-changing benefits. Ten to Zen can be done anywhere, at any time, and by anyone—its beauty lies in its practicality and simplicity. It is so straightforward to learn that anyone can make it a part of their daily life. In fact, Ten to Zen is not only easy and effective, but also one of the best investments of time you are ever likely to make.

## Why "Zen"?

So why did I call it "Ten to Zen"? What images come to mind when you think about reaching a state of "Zen"? Some of you may think of Zen Buddhism, the spiritual path. Others may see Zen in a more general sense, as a kind of shorthand for relaxation.

From the outset, I should explain that this book isn't based on Zen Buddhism. I don't focus on pure meditation or the road to enlightenment. I won't be using any gongs or chanting and there is no need to subscribe to a spiritual practice. Rather, I am using the term in a colloquial way that is more to do with being "in the zone" or "chilled out." It's about achieving that highly desired state of mind that people often access through meditation, when we become calm, aware, and enlightened. It's about being focused yet relaxed: the idea of "Zen" as an approach to life that emphasizes creativity, simplicity, and intuition rather than fixating on goals. It's "Zen" in the sense of relaxation, of achieving that coveted sense of deep, centered calm.

Although this book isn't about Buddhism, my hope is that in honoring the wisdom in the teachings of Buddhism, mindfulness and psychology, alongside the wisdom of the dying and my experiences in therapy, you might find your own enlightenment in these workouts: your personal Zen, whatever that means for you.

I have been practicing this method and running workshops for many years, and I can promise you that if you follow the stages in this book, you will quickly learn to access this sought-after state of relaxed, calm focus, as and when you need it.

## Influences from the Living

As well as everything I share with you based on years of professional experience, I am no stranger to occasional challenges in my own life, and I'll be sharing some of these with you, too.

As I mentioned, as a therapist I hear much about how distressing life can be, and the concept of time often plays a prominent part in this. Not having enough time, wasting time, the passing of time—these are all common themes. I also hear many stories of chaotic lives and minds, of people lacking compassion for themselves and struggling to find ways to cope with the daily demands of life.

I have discovered over the years that no matter what therapy, workshop, or breathing technique is offered to an individual, it is far less effective if the person's level of distress is too high to process the techniques they are being shown. They simply cannot engage properly with the therapy or technique because there are so many other things going on for them, cluttering up their mental space.

Turning down the volume of the mind might be an easier way to think of this. My book is not a therapy program, but I hope that using the techniques and concepts in it will enable your brain to settle and become quieter, allowing you to enter a place where whatever is going on your life starts to feel more manageable.

The reality is, we are all in this together. We are all here on earth for an unknown period of time with a largely unknown life to live. That's the beauty of it. But if we are truly honest with ourselves, how often do we really live fully?

### Take a Moment . . .

So to start, let me ask you two simple questions. Sit quietly with your eyes closed for a minute and ask yourself:

1. Am I truly living the life I want?
2. Does my mind often feel peaceful and calm?

If you answered "no" to either or both of the questions, then welcome to the human race. Secondly, congratulations on making the choice to read this book. I'm not a mind reader, but if you have picked up this book, I imagine you are struggling with certain aspects of your life. What I can promise you—ultimately—is that taking a little time out of each day to follow my Ten to Zen mind workout, will make the positive difference you need.

# How This Book Works

The book is divided into two parts. Part 1, Chapters 1–3, gives you a sense of how the brain usually works, some of the research and reasoning behind the program and why I broke it down into ten minutes a day.

Part 2, Chapters 4–10, is roughly divided up into the "minutes," or steps, that correspond to the "minutes" in the workout. The full workout is summarized toward the end of the book on page 160, which will act as a prompt once you have worked through each chapter.

In Part 1, I have interspersed some of these "minutes," or steps, with general meditations and psychological exercises, which act as a kind of preparation to the ten-minute workout. These short exercises are flagged with the invitation to "Take a Moment . . ." and they are all part of the workout. They will guide you on how you can be kinder to yourself, deal with unpleasant emotions, and generally clear some of the unwanted mental baggage we all carry around with us so your mind will be freed up and able to get to the "Zen" bits much more quickly. You can think of it as a kind of mental decluttering. I've also included several case studies and sto-ries from my therapeutic experience. (All names or circumstances within the book have been changed to protect anonymity.)

I want to say from the outset that you don't need to be rigidly bound to the ten-minute time frame, and that different people will relate more or less to different exercises and aspects of the workout. Some find that they want to spend more time on mindfulness, others on the breathing. Please feel free to concentrate on parts that you particularly relate to and to make this workout as bespoke as you want. Having said that, I do recommend that you read through the whole workout initially. Once you feel comfortable with the entire thing, you can start to play around with it a little and ultimately decide what works best for you.

At the heart of my workout is the idea of bringing the mind's anxiety down, notch by notch, until the brain gets enough space to be able to think more clearly. I can't promise that practice will make it perfect, but it will certainly make it easier.

I am also going to talk a bit about the neuroscience behind the workout, especially in the early chapters, because I believe it's important you can see that everything I put forward is grounded in solid research. Also, I believe that techniques often work more efficiently when people understand *why* they work. However, I'm not going into the neuroscience too much because, although it provides the framework for the workout, it is just one part of it (and I don't want to scare you off). Alongside this framework there is another layer, which I broadly term "principles for living," and I will go into these in the later chapters.

So to really get the most from the book, it is important to read through the preliminary chapters first. You can skip them and go straight to the workout itself, but you won't get as much out of it that way.

# Your Mind May Be Running the Show

I'm aware that many of you can justifiably name any number of factors that prevent you from living fully or having a calmer mind, such as money worries, relationship issues, noisy neighbors, or other factors that contribute to uncomfortable feelings. Perhaps you have a bullying boss, or difficult things have happened to you in the past that cause you anxiety.

These are all valid concerns. But have you ever stopped to consider how your mind, with its amazing ability to process and interpret life's events, can have a considerable influence on *how* you live and experience your life?

The reality is that it does, and not always in a helpful way. In fact we know from neuroscience and psychology research (the "sciences of the brain") that what goes on in our minds impacts every aspect of our experience.

Often, our minds run riot if they are not looked after properly. I find it very interesting that we pay attention to every other organ of the body, especially if we detect a problem or identify a need for maintenance, but we often ignore our minds. It's as if we just expect them to take care of themselves, as if everything that happens there is on autopilot. While there is some truth in this, we also have a lot of control over our thoughts, and instigating a daily mind workout is a great way to start exercising and strengthening this control. This is where Ten to Zen comes in. It's designed to help you live a more balanced life and avoid becoming a prisoner of the antics of your mind.

# Ten to Zen: The Ultimate Benefits

Many self-help books I've read make promises to change your entire life. Not this one. I can't change the circumstances of your life, but I can help you decide how you respond to them. I can offer you some tools that can enable you to change your unhelpful responses to more helpful ones. I can promise that if you engage with what is on offer here, it will change how you see life and give you the chance of living with more hope.

Ten to Zen is based on my years of experience and professional training, but also on a common-sense approach gained from observing what actually works for people.

All the therapeutic grounding techniques I use are supported by scientific research that shows how effective they are and how they benefit the mind. Rather than drown you in quotes from hundreds of articles, I'm just going to summarize broadly what we know happens when we calm down, deactivate the mind's threat system, get some mental space, and simply treat ourselves a little better:

- MRI scans show positive changes in our brains, including better stress management and improved mental functioning.

- Our physical health improves, alongside our healthier minds.

- Our relationships improve.

- We become more productive and creative and take less sick leave.

* Our view of the world changes.

* We cope better with life and become calmer.

* We become happier.

In other words, we start to live rather than just exist. I sincerely hope on our journey together that you opt in to living fully rather than just existing, and make the changes in your life that you deserve.

## About Me

Now you know a little about my professional background it might be useful to know a little bit about me as a human being.

I live with my long-term partner, Mark, and we have a dog called Kate. Kate teaches us a lot about living calmly—if you truly want to learn how to hit the "pause" button and regain perspective, I suggest that you watch a dog chill out sometime. In my eyes, they are the masters of Zen.

As well as regular walks with Kate, I like to run because it clears my head. I'm no athlete, but I have run a few marathons. There's a reason I mention running here. Every time I've run a marathon I've brought my transit card with me, just in case I need to catch a train home at the halfway point! In my view, completing a marathon is linked more to mental stamina than to physical. In the past, I've had moments when sheer exhaustion made me think of quitting. Then it was the stopping to pause, breathe, regain focus, sort out my head, and then get on with it again that got me over the finish line.

Now I can see that I was practicing a kind of Ten to Zen before I had really developed the concept! Probably lots of you are already doing this, too. For many of us, life these days can feel like a never-ending marathon, so finding those moments to pause and rebalance has never been more important. That way, we can pace our "life marathons" more comfortably.

## A Touch of Common Sense

I hold the firm belief that when it comes to healthy mental well-being, a common-sense approach is essential. I don't want this to be a heavy, dull read. I want it to be clear and accessible, so I'm trying to keep it simple while also providing enough background information to show that the practices are grounded in scientific research.

Complex theories, endless analysis, and an ongoing quest for deeper psychological significance may be what some people require, but it doesn't work for everyone. I don't judge or criticize colleagues who adopt such approaches in therapy, as sometimes they are absolutely essential. But this is not the purpose of my book. I am more interested in helping people function better on a daily basis, understand the workings of their minds a little more and simply bring down their distress levels a few notches.

As therapists, we can sometimes make the mistake of using academic theory–driven language that confuses people. I believe that we need to listen more carefully to what our clients want—and that, in my experience, is simply to feel better. A clear, realistic, scientifically researched and time-efficient tool works, not just for ten minutes, but as a way of life. It's like having a messy garden. If you don't take time out on a regular basis to tend to your garden, soon the weeds will set in. Our brains need similar daily maintenance so that things don't start to feel out of control and we can create the time we need to attend to any chaos.

Ten minutes each day is what this program asks for and if, in time, people want to practice for longer, or use the techniques at different times of the day or night, then that is a bonus. I believe that it would benefit all of us if we adopted a more proactive approach to looking after our mental well-being to help prevent the tougher times from feeling overwhelming. These experiences can be periods of great growth and learning, if only we allow them to be. As my mother used to say, "You can't appreciate summer unless you've experienced winter."

So, let's get started on your Ten to Zen adventure. It has changed my perspective on life and that of the many people I have worked with. Today is the day you will start to take care of your mind. It is a new beginning.

You won't look back. I am glad you have joined me.

PART ONE

# THE BACKGROUND

# CHAPTER 1:

# The Ten in the Zen

A few years back, I worked in private practice with a lady I'll call Jane.

Jane worried endlessly about numerous matters, and as part of her treatment I suggested thirty minutes of pure mindfulness meditation every day. I provided her with a recording and all the relevant instructions. Jane had never meditated in her life, and after several weeks of this she came to a session in quite an irritated mood. When I explored with her the cause of her agitation, she told me bluntly it was my meditation suggestion:

"I have four kids, a full-time job, and an alcoholic husband, and you're telling me to relax and practice mindfulness for thirty minutes a day," she said. "This isn't working for me. I'm too stressed and busy to meditate!"

I squirmed in my seat, and something fundamentally shifted for me. As someone experienced in meditating and taking "time out" for myself, I was guilty of assuming it would be easy for other people. The reality is, mostly it's not. Jane was a forceful reminder that most of us don't have the time to meditate for half an hour every day, or a few spare days to go on a retreat. So I started to think about creating something that would work fast.

I began to notice that many self-help and psychology books, courses, and seminars also involve a lot of time and commitment. It's widely accepted that therapy itself can be time-consuming and costly. However, for a lot of people time and money are limited, and committing to more detailed programs simply isn't an option. It's why I unapologetically developed a workout for the mind that is accessible, realistic, and highly effective in a very short period of time. It's as simple as that.

Jane needed a time-efficient program that was realistic for even the busiest person. It occurred to me that just about everyone manages to find ten minutes in their day to brush their teeth and take a shower. So I set about trying to find a simple way we can care for our minds in the same way as we take care of our bodies, maybe taking a little less time, but definitely doing it much more often. This acknowledgment that most people find it a challenge to take more than ten minutes out of their day to focus on meditation or breathing mindfully is at the core of my technique, and why it works.

# Creating Mental Space

I also realized that Jane needed to reduce the levels of distress and threat she was feeling before it would be possible for her to find the mental space she needed in order to breathe and reflect. We've probably all experienced times when we've been feeling distressed and someone says something like, "Don't worry, just take a few deep breaths and it'll be OK." It's a kind sentiment, but the reality is, your brain may need a little more help than this to soothe itself quickly. My Ten to Zen solution sets out a specific, structured guide to slowing down the activity of the mind, and creating this necessary mental space.

# What's in the Ten Minutes?

Ten minutes may not seem much in terms of time, but I have packed a deceptive amount of valuable information into those minutes. Ten to Zen has two main layers:

* The "foundation" layer, which comprises the practical skills such as breathing, meditation, and mindfulness—the tools you will need to perfect your practice.

* The "top" layer, which I loosely refer to as your Ten to Zen "principles for living"—these will become part of your daily routine and can be used whenever works for you.

The practical skills will help slow down your mind, restructure how you think, and enable you to adopt a more adaptable approach to your day.

The principles of living involve making and embodying certain key commitments, based on the principles of compassion, acceptance, and authenticity. I like to think of them as being rather like an invisible "mental cloak" that I put on every morning to help me face the day. Each day you will be putting on that mental cloak during your Ten to Zen time, as both a reminder and a commitment to yourself.

Both these aspects—practical skills and principles for living—are based on skills, techniques and principles from the therapeutic worlds in which I have trained. These include mindfulness, cognitive behavioral therapy (CBT), eye movement desensitization and reprocessing (EMDR), and interpersonal and compassion-focused therapies. All these approaches have very positive outcomes for helping people live happier lives.

Let me explain briefly the core principles of each therapy:

- **Mindfulness** is about living in the present moment and not becoming too attached to your past or the future.

- **Interpersonal and compassion-focused therapies** acknowledge how we relate to ourselves and to others while learning how to treat ourselves and others with greater compassion and kindness.

- **Tapping** is an effective technique used to help people become more grounded and quickly get to a safe place where things can quiet down and the mind's threat system can be managed. (It is also known as bilateral stimulation and is sometimes used as a grounding, calming technique in EMDR, a therapy used to treat trauma.)

• **Cognitive behavioral therapy** focuses on the connection between how we think and how we feel. We will be using techniques from the world of CBT to learn to let go of unhelpful thinking patterns.

I decided to extract techniques from these therapies because they can calm and settle the mind quickly in a safe, controlled manner. Remember, Ten to Zen is not therapy, but a mind workout that allows your mind to settle down quickly so you can function better. In essence, it can make you calmer and more focused, enabling you to become your own therapist when necessary.

## Why I Use CBT and Mindfulness

I use mindfulness and CBT because I believe that our thoughts can often be the "demons" in our lives, creating a lot of mental pain. And we all naturally do with mental pain what we do with physical pain—we try to dampen it down, to nullify it. In fact, this pain is usually telling us something very important and we should be paying attention to it. As a therapist, I often see people trying to run away from or bury their difficult emotions, whereas I believe they should see them more as signposts. These more difficult or challenging emotions can be a route to personal clarity, and ultimately to finding real happiness. I address this by acknowledging that we sometimes need to move toward difficult thoughts and emotions, initially just letting them be until we can make sense of them, before we can make a decision on what we can then let go of.

As I have said, this book is different from other books because it's not just giving you a practical tool kit—such as meditations, mindfulness, and so forth—although that is one aspect of it. There's a lot more to Ten to Zen than that, such as helping you explore your values, your principles, and how to live authentically. In the following chapters I will be going into more detail about exactly how each stage works. However, I'll give you a flavor of what this looks like now so you don't start to become impatient. (Not ideal when one is trying to find calm!)

The practical part of your ten minutes will include the following:

- **Stopping** the train of thought that is causing you distress

- Using **mindfulness and interpersonal psychotherapy** to check in on what's going on with you

- Using **therapeutic techniques** to bring the chatter of the mind down a notch and slow down the mind's activity, thereby creating a safe place for you to stop and breathe

- Using **breathing techniques for mind and body** to bring the mind down another few notches to a calmer state

- Decluttering any unhelpful thinking through **cognitive behavioral therapy**

- Using **mindfulness and present-moment awareness** to clear away any mental fog

- Donning your invisible **Ten to Zen "mental cloak,"** which represents your principles of self—**compassion, acceptance, and authenticity**

- Going on to face your day with **awareness, courage, and hope**

Finding time to pause is a challenge for many people, but it's not impossible. And this isn't just about pausing. This is about stopping to recharge our brains in the most helpful of ways. I want the ten minutes you spend on Ten to Zen to be a practical and useful part of your day that will change how your brain functions and how you live your life.

The "mental cloak" I mention will be explored in Chapter 9. For now, it is enough to know that the psychological techniques to slow the mind down need more than just practical skills. Your Ten to Zen "mental cloak" should be donned every day because it will offer alternative guidance that will help you when challenges emerge or when your mind acts up, telling you that you are worthless, pathetic, or weak. As part of the Ten to Zen workout, you will nurture a kinder voice toward yourself.

Ten to Zen works. Yet the workout is far more than just the techniques. It is a new way of living and a fresh approach to how we treat others and ourselves.

# CHAPTER 2

# Committing to Change

Recently I worked with a young man in his late twenties whom I'll call Joe. Joe is a bright, intelligent young man with a dry sense of humor. His main issue was that he wanted to develop his confidence and feel less worried. Therapy was a tough process for Joe, as he had lots of difficult life events to make sense of. One day in session Joe asked me, with a slight smirk on his face, if there was an easier option for helping him cope better with his life. When I probed a little more, his response made me smile: "Don't you have anything you can offer me that doesn't involve me having to do any of the work—like a ready-made version?"

We laughed a little, and it won't surprise you that Joe was informed that, sadly, there are no ready-meal versions for change. Change can take time, and Joe needed to spend time each day on the major changes he wanted to make before things really started to shift.

However, Joe was soon able to use the techniques of living I taught him to bring about significant positive changes in his life. It wasn't an easy road and at times he was outside his comfort zone. Yet he moved from a belief that he was "a nobody" to a belief that he was of value and his voice did matter, so much so that eventually he embarked on a life-long ambition to study as a journalist.

## Making a Conscious Commitment

Wanting to change is not the same as making a real commitment to doing so. This brings me to another time, when I was in London on a cold winter's day, delivering a Ten to Zen workshop to a corporate business. As always, I started with a light introduction and invited participants, if they felt comfortable, to share how they experience life generally. Mary kicked off with an all-too-familiar description:

"I just feel like I'm drifting through life on autopilot, with no real sense of purpose, passion, or direction. I have regular moments when I become overwhelmed, can't think clearly or make decisions. My mind is like an enemy that's often critical, negative, judgmental, and just thinks the worst. On top of this I'm stressed—and feeling tired, both physically and mentally, most of the time."

Fortunately for Mary, this ten-minute mind workout helped her gain insight into how her negative thought patterns were sabotaging her happiness. Once she realized this, she was able to start changing how she lived and coping with the demands of her life. Creating time and space every day to follow the Ten to Zen workout opened her eyes to a new way of thinking and experiencing, which in turn led to monumental changes in her life.

If anything in Mary's description resonates with you, then it is time for you to wake up and consider changing. Living like this is not living life fully. It is existing uncomfortably. Remember, you do have a choice about this. I invite you to *stop* now and take just one minute for our next exercise.

 **Take a Moment . . .**

Do you truly want to change and live a fuller, calmer life, rather than just carrying on existing uncomfortably?

Make a brief note here, or in a notebook, of your thoughts and any other feelings that came up while you reflected.

If you answered yes to my question, great. This could be a huge step forward for you. (If you answered no, keep reading anyway. I might just change your mind!) Before we move on though, just a brief word on change.

## Change Can Take Time

Real change takes time. It requires commitment and can feel a little daunting at first. Change can be uncomfortable because it encourages us to move out of our comfort zones. The fearful aspect of our nature encourages us to resist change and hide under the duvet, but in your Ten to Zen workout I will be encouraging you to embrace change with open arms. It is through taking the risk to change that you will allow countless new possibilities in your life to emerge. You are not alone in this. Like everyone else reading this book, you are trying to make sense of things that can sometimes feel senseless. Take comfort from knowing that you are among a like-minded community of Ten to Zen people, all deciding not to accept a life of just existing, but moving toward embracing a life lived fully.

It all starts with you and there will be a few requirements.

 **Take a Moment . . .**

Here's another question for you to think about:

Are you willing to commit to ten minutes each day to embark on your Ten to Zen journey?

# Why It's Called a Workout

Here's the deal from my perspective. If what I am saying makes sense to you, then the very act of your opting in and committing to the Ten to Zen workout will start to make a difference. I have deliberately called this a workout because that's exactly what it is—a mental workout to help the mind function in a way that truly enhances your life. It works in a similar way to a physical workout—if you don't show up at the gym on a regular basis, and perhaps improve your diet, too, then your body won't change.

Our brains are no different. We will be training the mind, strengthening it, and helping it develop flexibility—just as we do our bodies. Remember, though, you do need to show up. This is not just about knowing what to do in theory; this means putting the theory into practice. The contractual agreement I need from you is that you will opt in, when you are ready. This means not only committing to, but also prioritizing, the ten minutes as an essential component to your day. After all, my guidance and the content of this book are one part of the deal; the second part is over to you.

So the question is, do we have a deal?

# Make Your Commitment

If so, I invite you do something very simple:

 **Take a Moment . . .**

Stop for one minute now, close your eyes, and take a few breaths. Create a short sentence, unique to you, that describes your contractual agreement to give this workout a try and to start taking ten minutes out each day to care for your mental well-being.

If it helps, here is mine:

"I commit to showing up for myself every day and looking after my mind with kindness."

Write your personal contractual agreement to yourself here, or on a card. You may want to take a photo of it for your phone, to remind you of your commitment throughout the day:

## How This Helps

It may be helpful to hear from someone who benefited from making this simple commitment. Peter is a private client of mine who gets quite stressed when he has to fly for work purposes. A while back, he described an occasion when a flight was turbulent and he became highly anxious: "My mind started to tell me several stories on the journey about potential accidents, or a hijacking, or worrying if the pilot has forgotten to turn on the seat-belt sign. My heart was racing, I was sweating, and I just wanted to get off."

Needless to say, none of Peter's stories had any basis in reality. But he was able to use techniques from his Ten to Zen practice to help him stand back from his worry and see that his mind was catastrophizing (jumping to the worst-case scenario). The use of tapping and breathing techniques, which we will explore in Chapters 5 and 6, immediately made him feel more at ease within a fearful situation. Now he even manages to enjoy flying, knowing he can use these techniques whenever he becomes fearful or anxious. He has learned how to turn down the volume of worried thoughts in his mind and return to more rational, helpful thinking.

Using the Ten to Zen workout enables people to manage circumstances that they find anxiety-provoking or challenging by promoting feelings of safety and control. If you ever feel anxious in certain situations (and most of us do), then taking time out to follow what I offer here may help considerably. There may even be times when you are uncertain why you feel stressed or worried, but the feelings are present nonetheless. Essentially, our minds often operate in "threat mode," not always helpfully, so the goal is to switch off this threat mode when it is not needed. Deactivating it instantly brings a sense of ease and calm, leading to clearer thinking. (I will be explaining this in more detail in the next chapter.)

## Taking Care of Our Minds

It fascinates me how often we fixate on how we look, what we wear, our work, how much we earn, and so on, but our minds barely get a second glance. Yet our minds are often the epicenter for much of the distress we experience. Let's face it: at times our minds are operating like a manic group of trapeze artists jumping from one worry to the next, at a pace that would embarrass most Olympians.

A few times in my own life I have experienced particularly difficult periods—bereavements, relationship disappointments, or struggles with the relentless demands of life. Alongside all the normal challenging emotions that go with such periods, I discovered that my brain seemed to be heightening certain emotions. My brain's "threat center," otherwise known as the amygdala, seemed to become overactive. While I was trying hard to process all my emotions, my amygdala was working equally hard in a most unhelpful way. The point here is that whatever is going on in your life right now, your brain may not always be working in your best interest.

Each person reading this book will have their own stories involving issues such as loss, rejection, abandonment, and whatever other trials life has dealt. However, *these are stories of your life and they don't define who you are; they can only shape who you are depending on how you to choose to respond to them.*

We've all heard the phrase "My mind was playing tricks on me." Well, your mind may be doing all sorts of things that you are currently unaware of, such as deleting inconvenient truths or aggravating or catastrophizing others. In everyday life, this can play out in many different ways:

- That funny look your boss gave you may not have meant you are being fired.

- Your partner may still love you as much as ever, despite the fact they forgot to text you yesterday.

- The failure you have just experienced may not mean you are entirely useless.

- The fact your teenage daughter told you at breakfast she "hates" you probably means "only for a moment," rather than for ever and always—she will probably tell you she loves you in half an hour.

- The barista in Starbucks who looked at you today like you were asking for a kidney transplant, when all you wanted was a cappuccino, may not actually have disliked you and was probably just having a bad day.

Sometimes our brains need a little downtime—just as our bodies need rest during the day—to help us regain perspective. Equally, we need to understand why we are responding in the way we do, to help us shift that perspective.

This book is about helping you do that so that you can start to live in a way that is calmer, more peaceful, and ultimately more adaptable. Ten minutes each day is nothing, I am sure you will agree, for such enormous benefits.

 **Take a Moment . . .**

Let me ask you another question:

How often do you stop to pay attention to your mental well-being and maintenance?

Stop now for just a moment and think about this.

What was your answer?

I'm going to guess that for most of you the answer is "never," "hardly ever," or "not often enough" because "I don't have time." If that's the case, welcome, welcome, welcome. You may answer this question very differently once you begin to experience the advantages of committing to real change.

There is no getting away from the fact that a brain that is not looked after can run riot and lead to many detrimental consequences. My professional knowledge, experience, and passion have shown me that we all need to try to understand our minds a little more and treat them with great care. We also need to change how we relate to ourselves, and treat ourselves with more kindness and compassion. Care of our minds and compassion to ourselves change everything beyond measure.

So, buckle up, get comfortable with the beautiful mess it is to be human, and join me on this journey of reclaiming a quieter mind in just ten minutes every day. You are now on the road to change.

# CHAPTER 3:

# The Antics of the Brain

I'd like to start this chapter with a story from a delegate at one of my workshops. John confessed that he had a tendency to always think the worst in any situation. One time, he brought his mother to the hospital for a checkup because she was experiencing pain in her stomach. While the doctor was assessing her, John decided to go for a coffee. When he returned, his mother was no longer in the exam room, and he asked the doctor where she was. The doctor replied that she had gone, at which point John fell to the floor in tears, believing his mother had died. Seconds later, before the doctor had had a chance to explain, John's mother returned, proclaiming she was fine and much relieved that the doctor had diagnosed trapped wind. John's mind had also been producing some hot air, if you will pardon the pun. In that moment, his brain had quickly produced a very extreme narrative based on minimal information.

How often do we react to our mind's irrational storylines in a similar manner to John?

So before we get to the actual Ten to Zen workout, I'd like you bear with me and read through the next two chapters, because getting some understanding of how our brains work in times of stress will set you up to get the most benefit from your practice. I know, when some of us hear about brains or neuroscience, we may tune out. Trust me, understanding the workings of the mind will in itself create a sense of freedom, simply because you begin to understand that *you are not the content of your mind*. It's quite a liberating moment.

## The Hardwiring of the Mind

Our brains are rather like large blobs of jelly that act like computers or processors. They absorb a lot of information from the moment we are born. Essentially, in our formative years they tend not to differentiate too much about whether information they are given is true, reasonable, or fair; they simply absorb everything they receive via their experiences. This we have no control over.

Over time, our brains develop their plasticity. This is basically the brain's ability to strengthen and change over time, by developing flexibility or adaptability. When all goes to plan in the developmental years, this tends to happen reasonably successfully. However, life doesn't always go to plan, and the development of our brain's strength and flexibility may be interrupted if we have experiences that are very challenging or difficult.

Neuropathways (or we can call them circuits) also develop, which are rather like a complicated set of circuit boards set up to receive information from the peripheral nervous system to the brain, and also to connect different regions of the brain to each other. They help determine how information is passed along and processed. In case you start to worry that I've gone into scientist mode, let's keep it simple. If I suddenly fall and injure myself, my peripheral nervous system sends a message to my brain that I've been hurt. My brain will then activate my pain receptors and a chain of events is set in motion.

As our neuropathways develop, patterns of thinking, behavior, and reactions begin to emerge whenever something is triggered.

We are rather like very complex computers that receive a lot of information. Once we get the information, the wheels are set in motion for how the brain will operate in every aspect of our lives—how we think, feel, react, eat, drink, sleep, move, function, and so on. The list is endless, but essentially, it's how we live. Beyond this, good and bad events in life occur. Each event will trigger an automated learned response from our brain that in turn leads to the emotional consequences we experience.

The great news in all this is that we have a choice in whether we opt in to the unhelpful learned responses or not. I will explain how to do this later (see page 52). Another remarkable consideration is that each of our patterns will be different in some way, as we have all had different experiences.

# The Mind in "Threat Mode"

Let me say straight up, I am no stranger to a worried mind. Neither do I have any interest in hiding behind professional titles or behaving like a perfect guru. Like most of the human race, I struggle at times, but I have made a choice to try to grow as a result of my struggles, rather than be defined by them.

I grew up in Belfast in Northern Ireland in the 1970s and 1980s during the period that was known as The Troubles. This was a great training ground for understanding trauma, the anxious mind, and how to live with uncertainty. Bombings, shootings, and riots were commonplace. Yes, it was a scary environment to grow up in, but, thankfully, it was also a place full of laughter and some of the kindest people I've met. Thank you, Belfast, for that.

I came from a very working-class family, where there was a lot of love, but some difficult times, too. I also grew up Catholic. Before I talk more about that, I should say I have respect for the compassionate work that many religions or churches do. However, for me, there was a flip side. Being Catholic came with those familiar companions guilt and shame. My motto became "If it feels good, it must be bad." I slept in a bedroom with a statue of the Virgin Mary with luminous eyes watching me . . . I am sure you get the picture.

Then, as a teenager, I realized I was gay. This was certainly the icing on the cake as far as living with anxiety goes. Coming out in Ireland in those days was not easy; some people didn't understand a way of life that was seldom talked about. I can fondly remember when a sex scene between a man and woman appeared on television, my mother would jump in front of the television like a security guard, much to the entertainment of me and my brothers. It was many years before I plucked up the courage to tell them I wouldn't be kissing any women like those men on the television.

Because I was identified as different, I was bullied quite a lot as a teenager and was no stranger to regular humiliation. Difference, as I'm sure many of you will know, wasn't tolerated. As a result of all this, my brain became hardwired very early on to function under threat in order to protect myself. The anxieties I experienced growing up meant that the neuropathways in my brain developed in their own particular way.

This was the start of my understanding of what it is to be anxious. Some of you will have similar memories of how it feels to experience chronic levels of worry and distress at an early age. These early experiences shape our learned responses, influence our behavior and the choices we make, and have an impact on how we evolve in later life. The good news is that in committing to the journey you're about to embark on, you can start to rewrite the script. I did it—and you have the power within you to do it, too.

# Who's Directing Your Movie?

The mind sometimes appears to do its own thing. This is related, in part, to what I've just described around neuropathways, plasticity, and how our particular patterns develop. At times our minds will produce worries and fears or even misinterpret situations based not on what is actually happening outside in the real world, but on old patterns or habits that are in place. Sometimes the thoughts our minds produce make no sense whatsoever.

I often compare the stream of thoughts that run through our brains to a movie, and one that sometimes has no director or producer. Yet whatever is going on in this movie significantly impacts how we feel. Sometimes we can observe the movie in our mind, curious about the content, but then can quickly move on. We don't take it too seriously, and there are no drastic changes in our mood. However, on other occasions we decide to play a leading part. We step into the screen and get fully involved in the mind's "antics," which often negatively impacts our mood or level of worry. In fact, some of us become so involved in the mind's script that we could warrant an Oscar for Best Actor.

The problem is that all this involvement with the mind's "antics" eventually becomes exhausting and has negative consequences on our functioning. This is especially likely if the stories our mind is telling us are cold, harsh, judgmental, or self-deprecating, which is often the case. These stories may be learned, habitual patterns that are generated on autopilot, but in time they can become very familiar and start to feel like truths. Again, the good news is they are often false truths.

### 🕑 Take a Moment . . .

Stop reading for a moment and, if possible, close your eyes. Make a decision to observe what's going on in your mind at this very moment. Simply notice what your mind is doing. Is it planning ahead, looking back, judging, worrying? Is it maybe thinking over details of a particular event?

Make a few notes here, or in a notebook, on what you notice:

While you were observing this activity in your mind, was it an easy process to observe your thoughts? Were you able to just let them be, knowing they will pass rather like a cloud passing in the sky, or did you find yourself engaging with the thoughts and developing the story further? Make a few notes.

Again, there are no right or wrong answers here. I am only interested in helping you develop an awareness of how you relate to what goes on in your mind.

## You Have Choice and You Have Control

What most of us fail to recognize is that we have some choice in how we manage our minds. When they are behaving a little chaotically there are ways of regaining control. The techniques and principles of your daily Ten to Zen mind workout will enable you to do this and it's truly liberating. We have the choice of whether to opt in to the frenzy of the mind's activity or whether to retrain the brain to become quieter when it decides to act up—almost like disciplining a naughty child.

There has been some superb work done over the past decade in the worlds of psychology and neuroscience that helps us understand our minds and subsequent behaviors. I promised not to deliver lots of academic psychology in this book; however, some of the research that neuroscience and psychology offer is fascinating and warrants mention. Here is broadly what we know:

* A lot of the time there is a huge amount of activity going on in our minds.

* Sometimes, like the movie analogy described earlier, it can be chaotic and often it makes no sense.

- Some researchers tell us we have around sixty thousand thoughts per day and up to 80 percent of the content of these thoughts can be negative or repetitive.

- MRI scans show us that when our threat system is activated (often habitually or unnecessarily), a chain of events occurs in the mind and body, which creates a stress response.

- MRI scans also show us that when the mind is trained to be mindful (for example, through the techniques in this workout), the threat system in our mind is deactivated.

## Catastrophic Thoughts

Have you ever had moments when something difficult is going on or maybe you are in a challenging situation, and your mind's default mode automatically thinks of the worst scenario? This is often the case, and through my workshops I have seen that there are a few favorites that always emerge (some of which I can almost imagine as pop song titles):

- This is a disaster!

- This always happens to me!

- What's the point?

- I should just give up now.

- I will not survive this.

Do any of these sound familiar? If so, don't worry. It's just how your brain is automatically responding. Addressing this is part of the work we are doing together. Changing how you respond and setting up new patterns will help you build more helpful automatic responses. Remember John from the start of the chapter? Just because we think the worst has happened does not mean that it has.

## Racing Thoughts

Most of us have experienced waking up in the middle of the night with too many ideas and thoughts whizzing through our minds. These racing thoughts can feel like the equivalent of five or six people all talking at once, and it makes it impossible to properly grasp and follow one thought because of the "noise" from all the others.

 ### Take a Moment . . .

Stop for a moment again, but this time with an intention to be still and simply do nothing. This time, check in with your brain just to observe, with curiosity, what the speed of activity is in your head at the moment. Nothing more. How would you rate this speed of activity on a scale of one to ten (one being totally slow, quiet and calm; ten being absolute fast-lane chaos)?

Also, notice how your physical body feels in relation to the level of activity in your mind. Remember, at this stage you are just noticing and observing with a real sense of curiosity. Whether you rate one or ten isn't important for now; what is important is that you've noticed. Noticing is what will begin to make all the difference to your life and help you take back control.

Note down your mind-speed rating, as a number between one and ten:

Note down your physical reactions:

## Unusual Thoughts

Apart from the volume of thoughts or speed of their activity, have you ever had thoughts that make no sense or even seem a little unusual? Again, rest assured this is normal. Another thing we are prone to do is to tell ourselves that all this mind-wandering activity in our brains is "true" and that we need to respond to it now. This is not helpful if you are in the middle of a meeting at work and your brain wanders off to think about shopping for dinner. The boss is asking for the latest figures for the month and your reply is, "chicken pot pie." The brain is doing what it is supposed to do, wandering, but it may not be entirely helpful in that moment. I think we have all been there at some point.

So now you have a little insight into the way our thoughts can trick us and hold us hostage, it's time to look at how we can start to redress this.

## Taking Back Control

I'd like now to share a few minutes inside the mind of one of my clients, Susan, when she has had a particularly stressful morning:

Susan wakes at 8 a.m., an hour later than she planned to, because her alarm didn't go off. She needs to be in London for a 9 a.m. workshop she is leading, so her level of stress is already higher than normal. As she is showering, the story in her head tells her that she will be late, the workshop will be a disaster, and they will never invite her back.

However, moments later she notices a toy belonging to her dog in the bathroom, which reminds her that her dog has a vet's appointment later that day. She then starts to plan how she will get back home in time to get to the vet. The vet is close to a supermarket, which reminds her that she needs to order a cake for her husband's birthday.

She then goes on to wonder about the security guard who works in the supermarket, as she hasn't seen him for a few weeks. When Susan last saw him, he mentioned going back to Lagos to see his family. This then reminds Susan that she needs to book a flight to see her family in Scotland. She then starts to think about dates for her trip.

Then a knock on the bathroom door reminds Susan she is late for her workshop. Her head returns to the original story that she's going to be late and the entire workshop is going to be a disaster.

Quite a busy few minutes, I am sure you will agree.

Apart from the flurry of activity going on in Susan's head during these few minutes, it won't surprise you to read that there were also changes in her body. In her words:

"My chest was tight, my breathing was fast, my heart was pounding, my mouth was dry, and my head hurt. The more conscious I became of these symptoms, the more aggravated they became. In turn, these physical changes in my body seemed to be contributing even more to the volume of activity in my head and vice versa. Essentially, I was caught in a trap."

The issue with modern humans' brain is that, as we have evolved, the mind has become more sophisticated and busy. Our threat systems (also known as our fight-or-flight response) don't seem to want to switch off, which sets in motion an entire series of events in our minds and bodies.

## Understanding the Chaotic Mind

So what is going on with Susan?

- Susan awoke and became stressed when she realized she was late. Her fight-or-flight threat center (on the right-hand side of the brain, called the amygdala) was activated, saying "prepare for threat or danger." Think of the amygdala as an emergency alarm system that, when triggered, causes a chain of events physically and psychologically. This is a fantastic system that is extremely useful in an emergency or genuine crisis; in the event of actual danger or threat, it gives us the necessary energy and adrenaline we need to help protect us from harm. However, when it goes off out of context, or is exaggerated, or simply starts working on autopilot, it becomes problematic.

- In Susan's late-wake-up scenario, this state of threat activated a host of physical and psychological reactions that led to the flurry of activity in her brain and body. Everything was on high alert, and her brain began operating at top speed.

- Her brain is doing what it thinks it should be doing—reacting to a threat—but because the threat has been taken out of all proportion, it's not actually helping Susan. In addition to all of this, hormones such as cortisol and adrenaline also increase, which adds to the sense of imminent danger or threat. Her body is preparing her to wrestle with a tiger, but she's only late for work! This is because when activated or put on high alert, the amygdala also releases hormones such as cortisol and adrenaline, which in turn make some systems in the body work harder and faster. If you have ever experienced fast heartbeat, rapid breathing, or tummy churning when feeling distressed, this is probably what is happening. It won't harm you, but the brain thinks it's helping you when often it's not. It is a programmed response known as sympathetic nervous system activation. Essentially, it is a warning system alerting you that danger may be lurking.

* This in turn sets in motion a sense of urgency or threat. The brain and body must protect themselves or get away, which is when our minds start to go into overdrive with an avalanche of thoughts, concerns, and worries. It is an exhausting process, which most people feel they have no power over.

Does this sound familiar to you?

## Breaking the Anxiety Loop

The problem is that if all this activity is left unnoticed, our brains tend not to regulate or filter any of it. Susan gets stuck in an anxious loop. Her mind goes around in circles and it's all made worse because she makes the mistake of attending to each worry as it arises.

Thankfully, there is a solution for this that helped Susan to manage similar situations subsequently. This was simply to recognize what was going on in her mind, stop and pause, and use the Ten to Zen techniques to slow down both mind and body, thereby returning to a sense of perspective and sanity. She was able to break the loop.

## Switching Off Your Threat System

The techniques and principles you will learn are going to help switch off this threat system quickly and effectively. *Remember, if something has been activated, it can normally be deactivated, too.* On this occasion, the Ten to Zen workout enabled Susan to function effectively and gain control of the runaway train that was her brain.

It is very empowering to know that you have the techniques you need to pause, stop, and deactivate your runaway thoughts and so regain a sense of control in your life. Simultaneously, you deactivate the sympathetic nervous response (see page 50) and welcome in the parasympathetic nervous response, which is simply about slowing things down. Think of it almost like an accelerator and decelerator. In switching off the threat center, you can simultaneously activate other parts of brain that may be more helpful in regulating attention, emotion, and self-awareness. Researchers tell us that people who use mindfulness every day strengthen this part of the brain, which helps regulate and balance things out more. This in turn sets off a release of more calming, "feel-good" chemicals, such as dopamine and serotonin, which creates a sense of ease and control.

## So Let's Give It a Try

Whatever our circumstances, we will all have something going on right now that we are struggling with. It's the nature of our humanity. How our brain manages these challenges is often an issue, with thought patterns containing judgment and overthinking, and criticism taking center stage. Let's dip our toes into this new way of living by trying out this short activity:

 ## Take a Moment . . .

Take one minute to focus on something in your life that may be stressing or bothering you a little at the moment (not a huge life event at this stage, but a stressful irritation). Before pausing with this situation in mind, the only decision I want you to make is that you won't try to control what's going on, and just allow it to be.

Close your eyes, sit comfortably, let the thought of the situation just be in your mind and simply hold it there. Do nothing but breathe, normally.

Essentially, you are *leaning in* toward whatever is bothering you. You are not trying to block, stop, or push it away, but bringing it into your present-moment awareness. Present-moment awareness is a little like allowing a light to shine on whatever is going on in your life. It's a gentle, comforting light that can bring an immediate sense of ease or clarity. Learning to stay present in the here and now is something you will hear more about later. It will help enormously with quieting the antics of the mind.

Make some brief notes, here or in your special note-book, of what you notice. How did you feel about the situation after taking a moment to pause?

What was going on in your mind?

What did you notice in your body?

Remember, there are no rights or wrongs here; you are simply curious about getting to know your mind more and moving toward what is troubling you, rather than running away from it.

# None of This Is Your Fault

I want to emphasize here that we have no choice over what information is inputted into our brain in our developmental years. Yet, just as we know some personality types may, for example, be more prone to worry, we also know that the information that has been given to our brains when we are growing up has a significant impact on how we will respond to certain situations in everyday life.

The brain we have today is a product of our genetic make-up and the information it was fed in our developmental years. If life is a struggle sometimes for you now, as an adult, *it's not your fault*.

The reality is, many of us live with very self-critical scripts constantly playing out in our minds, making us doubt our worth and value. Please stop for a moment and sit with this thought: *it's not my fault*. Often we tell ourselves we are to blame, which I believe is one of the most painful lies we ever tell ourselves and the root of much distress.

 **Take a Moment . . .**

Stop now for a moment to think over the idea that whatever story your critical brain is telling you, or whatever antics your brain is currently up to, *it's not your fault. Truly. You did not program your brain.*

Again, note what thoughts and feelings come up and simply allow them to be. There are no right or wrong reactions. (Don't be surprised if you feel a little emotional acknowledging that it's not your fault.)

Recognizing that none of the early programming you received was your fault can be liberating because it is a step toward no longer feeling powerless and unable to do anything about it. Picking up this book is one encouraging sign that you refuse to stay powerless.

If you have been privileged enough to grow up in a society or family that has been mostly warm, safe, affirmative, and functional, without any key traumatic events occurring, then the likelihood is

- You are functioning well; or

- Your brain is probably functioning in a way that is helpful most of the time

In essence, your brain has been programmed to work in a way that is helpful for you. I am not suggesting life is perfect and that you won't experience challenges at times, but the way your mind responds to life events may be more adaptive than maladaptive.

However, if, like most of us, you have experienced some negative messages, adverse life events, and less-than-perfect families or social setups, then the chances are your brain may not always be working in a way that is best for you. Your brain has probably been programmed to automatically protect, defend, react, or view things through a more negative lens. However, that doesn't define who you are as a person.

# Flexibility Is Not Just Good for the Body

The likelihood is also that your brain's plasticity (the flexibility I mentioned earlier) may not be as robust as you might need it to be. Likewise, some of the neuropathway patterns (your circuit board) may have a few loose or faulty connections that get in the way of how information is processed.

If someone gets uncontrollably angry in certain situations, it could be that their mind has learned this response. That said, please don't read any of this information with a sense of despair—the fantastic news is that our brains can be reprogrammed to work in a way that is more effective for us. What has been learned can be unlearned.

So, the small boy who was told he was worthless, and too fat, or not good enough, who witnessed a drunk father beating his mother and was bullied at school more than likely has a brain that operates in threat and self-critical mode a lot of the time.

His brain has been programmed to fear and distrust. This is not his fault. He has experienced sad, unfortunate events and his brain has absorbed those experiences. Life is uncomfortable and he will probably have many negative beliefs about himself, others, and the world around him until he takes action to change (through Ten to Zen or other programs) and retrain his brain.

The little girl who was often left alone as a child, who was told she was ugly and stupid, who experienced abuse will likewise have a brain that operates mainly in threat and critical mode. This, too, is likely to continue into adulthood until she takes action. Her brain has been programmed to defend, protect, react, and withdraw. This is not her fault. She has had sad, unfortunate experiences and her brain has absorbed those experiences. Life is uncomfortable and she, too, is likely to develop many negative beliefs about herself, others, and the world until she takes action to change.

## That Old Chestnut, Shame

During my work with the dying, I often encountered people talking about shame. In the final stages of life they expressed shame around secrets, regrets, and wishes that things could have been different. And I also often witnessed people finally reach a place of peace when they were given the opportunity to talk about something that had caused them a sense of shame. The key was letting go.

Our dear old friend shame often gets neglected in self-help books, yet when your brain is operating in a constant state of shame, it can lead you to start believing the voice in your mind telling you that you are

- Less than

- Not good enough

- Worthless

- Unlovable

- Helpless

The list goes on. Shame has many definitions, but in my experience shame occurs when someone starts to fundamentally believe as truth what they have negatively experienced or been told. So their critical brain sends out a thought such as "You've failed again," and that begins to translate, in shame, into a belief that "*I am a failure*."

We have seen how our background and early experiences can influence our brains, which in turn influence patterns, triggers, thoughts, and emotions. These early negative experiences also often leave a residual sense of shame, which acts like a fuel that helps keep these patterns alive.

Shame is like mud that sticks and refuses to go away. Shame, in my experience, is the underlying catalyst for most human distress. Often this is not addressed adequately, which doesn't sit comfortably with me, as it's the one thing that will keep coming back until the person pays attention to its cries. Shame will unashamedly have a place at the table in your practice of Ten to Zen. It will be a much-welcomed guest, to be treated with compassion, acceptance, and openness.

## Take a Moment . . .

Take some time now to consider if you carry any sense of shame around with you.

Take a few moments now to identify any part of yourself around which you feel shame. I suggest a simple action, which is to sit for a moment with whatever that shame is, and welcome it in as a guest. The only action you are going to take is simply to be kind to yourself in this moment.

Describe what happened for you just now:

If you ever question whether you are good enough, are lovable enough, are worthwhile enough, or matter enough, then chances are you live with some degree of shame. Shame takes on many forms and guises but—like most things—it is learned, and thankfully it can be unlearned, too.

## Shame and Guilt—There Is a Difference

I can confidently say that shame has played a significant role in the struggles of almost every client I have ever worked with as a therapist. It is important to clarify that shame is different from guilt. If I treat someone disrespectfully or make a mistake in my life and then feel bad about the hurt

I've caused, I am experiencing guilt. This can be a helpful emotion. However, if I treat someone disrespectfully or make a mistake in my life and fundamentally believe I am a bad person as a result, then I am experiencing shame. Shame is toxic and needs to be faced courageously. Shame often cries out for some attention or recognition. Yet it is often ignored.

We often manage our shame unhelpfully by what I call the "Three Ss" approach:

- Keep it **Silent**

- Keep it **Secret**

- **Shout** it down

How does this look in real life? Well, on the day we are telling ourselves we are not good enough, we run away and try to distract or isolate. We criticize ourselves, or beat ourselves up in some destructive way. Maybe we'll get stuck on Facebook, Twitter, or any social media forum, where people describe wonderful lives, perfect families, fun times, and friends in abundance. Yet, ironically, loneliness surveys tell us people have never felt more isolated.

Within Ten to Zen I suggest an alternative 'Three As' approach to managing our shamed selves:

- **Attend** to it

- **Announce** it

- **Appreciate** it

Instead of silencing the difficult thought, we **attend** to it. Instead of keeping it a secret, we **announce** it (even if just to ourselves). Instead of shouting it down, we **appreciate** it. This, I passionately believe, makes all the difference to our lives. When we start to let go of shame-based behaviors, we begin to embrace ourselves in a way that is kinder, more compassionate, and more accepting. Remember that every one of us is struggling in some way and this imperfection is part of our humanity.

There is great freedom when we realize that the shame we've been programmed to feel doesn't have to be permanent. Ten to Zen can teach you how to quiet your mind to allow new information and experiences to be absorbed and replace your old, shame-based patterns with stronger, more adaptable ones.

A new way to live is just around the corner for you now that you have some understanding of the working of your mind. So let's get started on learning the techniques and principles that will now become a daily part of your day. The next chapter will look at the first two steps of your daily mind workout—stopping and checking in.

PART TWO

# THE TEN-MINUTE WORKOUT

# CHAPTER 4:

# Minute 1—Time to Stop

Last year I visited New York with my partner and some friends around Christmastime. One late afternoon we walked over Brooklyn Bridge toward the New York skyline. It started to snow, and the most beautiful view imaginable emerged. The wonder of the moment seemed almost to beg for everyone to stop; yet few did. As I stood there, truly lost in the moment, I suddenly felt sad watching people frantically moving on to their next destination. Stopping wasn't an option for them, yet stopping would have offered them, in that moment, so much magic.

It doesn't have to be a Brooklyn Bridge moment, but practicing Ten to Zen and committing to stopping for a short time each day will produce moments of delight, awareness, and insight beyond measure.

# Getting Started

By this stage you will have an understanding of some of the rationale behind this daily mind workout. We have explored these concepts:

- Why you might need Ten to Zen
- What the workout consists of
- What's required of you
- How you might benefit from it
- How our brains work
- How our minds don't always function in the most helpful ways
- The impact of shame

Now we arrive at the practical skills. Before we go any further I want to reiterate that, although learning this may take you a little time, putting it into practice will involve only ten minutes a day.

I'm sure you've gotten the message by now that this will not be ten minutes of stopping to do nothing or simply taking a breather or having a nap. It will be ten minutes of using highly effective, clinically researched techniques, from various psychology models, to slow down the processes of your brain and restructure unhelpful thinking. Again, I emphasize that the techniques are only one part of the workout, a means to clear the fog of the mind. Concurrently, you will embody a new way of relating to yourself, leaving you feeling much calmer and more in control. Although once you have learned the technique it is very simple to put into practice, initially it requires time, effort, and commitment.

I have deliberately designed these ten minutes in a very structured way, as I have found this to be the most helpful approach. These techniques can bring you to a place of stillness and clarity in a very timely manner.

Some of my clients like to view these ten minutes almost like going on a mini break, or having some relaxing downtime, with a clear structure and plan for each minute. To recap, this is what it looks like:

| | |
|---|---|
| Minute 1: Step 1. | Stopping |
| Minute 1: Step 2. | Checking in |
| Minutes 2 and 3: Step 3. | Arriving in a Zen-like, calm headspace |
| Minutes 4 and 5: Step 4. | Relaxing and slowing down in this space |
| Minutes 6 and 7: Step 5. | Finding new perspectives and ways of thinking |
| Minutes 8 and 9: Step 6. | Recharging |
| Minute 10: Step 7. | Gently coming back to the real world, ready to conquer whatever the day brings |

# What Is the Best Time of Day to Do This?

My recommendation is to practice at the start of the day, if possible. This helps to set the brain up to function in a more helpful way for the rest of the day. If you can create a sense of order in the brain at the beginning of the day, this will influence the remainder of your day in a positive way. This morning practice can also become a reminder that each time you practice you are subtly influencing how your brain functions.

For some of you, the start of the day will not be possible, so adapt the timing to whatever works with your routine and lifestyle. You may have particular times in your day that are always more challenging; they may be the times to engage with Ten to Zen.

For others, nighttime and getting to sleep may present challenges. If this is the case, then you can adapt and use the workout at bedtime, if this would be helpful for you.

In addition, you are not limited to ten minutes every day. If you need to use the workout at a few points during your day, to "dip in and out," so to speak, this can also be a sensible choice.

I want to avoid an over-prescriptive approach to this issue because I have faith that each of you will find a way to make this work. I encourage you to be mindful that the most important aspect in all this is making the initial commitment to stop. If Step 1, simply stopping everything else you are doing and "taking a moment," is not achieved, the rest becomes impossible.

However, I would like to add another word of caution

around tiredness. One of the mistakes people often make when using any form of meditative technique is to view the time as an opportunity to rest or to take a little nap. In fact the opposite should be true. This time is an opportunity to become fully awake and fully aware. If you find yourself becoming sleepy, make a conscious decision to adapt your posture to one that is upright, centered, and awake to new possibilities. I think of this as rather like making a decision to sit up straight when someone important enters a room. Likewise, in this workout it is important to tell yourself that you mean business when you enter into this time.

# Step 1—Simply Stopping

This chapter lays out for you the process of the first minute. My advice is to take each part slowly and stop and complete the exercises wherever possible. These techniques may need a little practice. During my workshops, we have a full day to draw together and practice all the techniques and principles. While using this book, just take everything one step at a time and move on to the next stage when you are ready.

## Planning When to Stop

Here are a few things to consider when you are planning how you are going to "stop":

- Can I commit to this time without fear of being interrupted?

- Will it be quiet enough or can I make the space quiet enough for the ten minutes?

Remember that you are stopping to let the engine of your mind cool down. This is a priority to prevent it overheating and burning out. Taking this time is making a decision to value yourself and take your mental well-being seriously.

Taking a little time to explore the concept of stopping at this stage of the book may seem unnecessary. However, not doing this would be like advising someone to go to the gym without sneakers. The stopping and the planning how to stop are both a must. This is not a skill that we in the Western world have mastered well.

The good news is that in making the decision to stop, you are halfway there. The rest will come naturally with practice. So wherever, whenever you stop, do the following:

- Commit to the time.

- Make sure you are in a comfortable space (if not, make it comfortable).

- Find a time you won't be interrupted.

- Keep an open mind.

- Know that the ten minutes will be of immense value to your life.

## Why You Should Stop, and No Excuses

The stopping, the deactivating, and the unplugging of whatever else you are doing, in the first moment, is key. When your brain is in threat mode, it can't take in the good information it needs. That's why I use the evidenced-based techniques I explained earlier, because just saying "Chill out" isn't going to trip the switch that gives the brain more room.

I'm not going to beat around the bush here. For most of you this first step—the stopping—will be the biggest challenge. The reasons for this will vary, but here are the top five excuses you may give for why you might have difficulty stopping:

1. "I'm too busy."

2. "There is nowhere quiet for me to go."

3. "Meditation or stillness don't work for me."

4. "I'm not sure this solution will work for people like me."

5. "I have other, more important priorities in my day."

I've heard them all before, countless times. Let me address each one individually:

1. Ten minutes each day is achievable for everyone. "Busy" can be an excuse to avoid change. Ouch! I know that's hard to hear, but fluffy words don't always inspire change.

2. There is always somewhere quiet to go; even if it's the bathroom wearing earplugs.

3. This is not just meditation or stillness. This is a mind workout that will quiet your mind so you can start to change how you live.

4. This solution works for most people. We are all human, with brains that have been proven to respond favorably to these kind of techniques.

5. There can be no greater priority than taking care of your mind.

I hope this seems reasonable. If I don't address these things now, you may find reasons not to do your practice or to delay it, which won't help you in any way. To be fair, I do acknowledge that stopping, apart from being a challenge practically, can also be a little frightening for some of us, as we may worry about what might "come up" in the stillness.

Try to rest assured that whatever comes up, you will almost certainly manage it. Furthermore, what has come up, whether it's a thought, an emotion, or a physical sensation, has done so for a reason and needs to be acknowledged. *(If, however, you do feel overwhelmed or something arises that you think may need expert help with, please do seek the opinion of a professional.)*

As I have said, when, where, and how you decide to stop is of course entirely your choice. The more important thing is to commit to doing this daily. Like brushing your teeth or going for a walk, the trick is to make it a daily practice.

# Step 2—Checking In

When we meet up with an old friend or someone we care about, often the first thing we do is ask them how they are. Sometimes this may just be a polite way to start a conversation, but if it's someone we are close to, we genuinely want to know. If the other person is happy, we can accept that. If they are sad or upset, we can also accept it and will normally reach out to support them in some way. The other person will, without doubt, feel better that we have taken an interest in them and, more importantly, have been able to accept them as they are in that moment.

Yet how the tables turn when it comes to ourselves, especially when we are struggling with "negative emotions." So I have a question for you: when was the last time you stopped to check in with yourself on how you are?

I'm going to guess this may not be as regular an occurrence as brushing your teeth. Isn't it fascinating that we value our teeth more than our minds? We could all have epitaphs on our tombstones reading, "Completely deranged but had lovely teeth." Good news for the dentists, and, of course, I'm fully supportive of good dental hygiene. But isn't it astounding how little time and attention we pay to our mental well-being?

Lack of care for the self is also a common feature of depression, about which I'd like to say a quick word. As you can see, I am passionate about healthy mental well-being and truly believe that a healthy mind leads to a happier life. I also believe that labelling people with broad diagnoses such as depression or anxiety is not always helpful.

The fact is, we all suffer at different times of our lives with changes in mood and levels of anxiety. Depression is never just depression; often worry, panic, and even obsessive traits become part of the mix. A healthier approach, I believe, is to acknowledge that we are all just human. Sometimes we struggle, sometimes we fall apart, sometimes we are lost or feel low, and sometimes we worry. But life can also be wonderful, adventurous, extraordinary, full of joy. I believe that we need to take the time to stop and appreciate the finer moments a bit more.

In the United Kingdom particularly, we are told to maintain a stiff upper lip in times of trouble and to get on with it. Yet it is questionable how helpful this really is. I can think of any number of clichéd expressions that get offered up in times of distress:

- "You just have to grin and bear it."

- "There's no point complaining."

- "Man up."

- "It could be worse."

- "There are people worse off than you."

It's almost as if there is a code of behavior that doesn't give us permission to check in on ourselves or express our difficulties. I think this issue is even more pertinent for men in a culture of "boys don't cry."

When I talk about checking in with yourself, I'm not advocating talking to yourself in front of the mirror or in public. Let's be honest, that could look a little odd and I don't want to be held accountable for anyone getting weird looks. Nevertheless, I am suggesting that the first minute of your Ten to Zen workout is devoted to checking in on how you are.

##  Take a Moment . . .

I assume now that you have stopped whatever else you were doing and are somewhere quiet and uninterrupted. This first step of your workout involves just sitting with your eyes closed with two intentions:

- Ask yourself how you're doing today. What feelings/emotions are around?

- However you are feeling today, accept completely that this is fine.

So how does that look within your daily workout? Sometimes identifying emotions can be a tricky business, with many of us fighting hard against uncomfortable emotions such as these:

- Sadness
- Anger
- Rage
- Jealousy
- Anxiety
- Frustration

We are usually more comfortable with positive emotions:

- Happiness
- Contentment
- Peacefulness
- Calm
- Excitement
- Love

Again, the list is almost endless. For now though, what happens when you check in with yourself? Are you aware of how you are at this very moment? Maybe now is a sensible time to pause and check in.

How are you really feeling?

# What If It Doesn't Feel Good?

"Negative emotions," as they are often termed, can come accompanied by a very lively commentator in our brains telling us these feelings are deserved, or wrong, or bad, or harmful, and should be pushed down at all costs. The commentator may even actively look for more evidence to support the negative thoughts, thus creating even more distress. The problem with this commentary is that it intensifies these emotions, and without fail, if they are not attended to, they will return. They are like that one very merry friend at a party who has overindulged in a sherry or two and won't leave you alone until you acknowledge them.

A lighthearted way to think about this internal chatter is to compare it to the two old men in *The Muppet Show* who sit on the balcony with a comment to make on everything. Get to know your commentator, but realize he or she isn't in charge. You don't have to listen to them or take them seriously. Your commentator is a pattern or a programmed response from your brain. As you know from Chapter 3, you don't need to opt in to listening to your critic or judge, now that you understand the human mind a little more.

Instead of terming these "negative emotions," I like to think of them simply as "human emotions," just like happiness or joy. They just have different lessons to teach us. There is no right, wrong, good, or bad. They simply identify a need in us at a particular time and we can use these emotions as an opportunity to grow if we attend to them by doing the following:

1. Acknowledging the emotion

2. Accepting the emotion

## Everything to Gain and Nothing to Lose

You may be asking yourself what the benefit is of this first minute of checking in. In my view, it is essential for beginning to quiet the mind and helping reduce any internal distress.

Have you ever had a situation when you felt upset with another person or worried they were upset with you? What happens when you don't address the problem? In most cases the situation festers or worsens and improves only when we actually address it. This is no different to how we relate to ourselves. The more we ignore our uncomfortable feelings, the worse they get.

Think for a moment how much energy goes into battling with these "negative emotions" or trying to hold on to the "positive emotions" when they arrive. Yet when we accept them as they are, regardless of what they are, there suddenly comes a sense of ease. There is nothing to battle. These feelings are not going to harm you and they certainly don't represent who you are. Acknowledging them, even welcoming them in and accepting them, is going to help to deactivate that overactive threat center in your brain.

So, the checking-in stage is exactly that—checking in with yourself to see what's going on in this moment. As simple as it sounds, turning toward the self in this first minute can bring an almost immediate sense of relief and calm. Suddenly you are not alone any more, as your "wise self" has turned up. Equally, you instantaneously create a sense of space between yourself and your emotions. A space to breathe and make sense of the moment. Already you are entering the early stages of a Ten to Zen state of calm.

If I haven't convinced you of the value of the first minute, then perhaps the evidence from studies, research, and brain scans will:

- As you move away from autopilot, the chaotic activity in your brain slows down.

- As your emotions are acknowledged and attended to, distress is reduced.

- When you have an awareness of being looked after, a sense of comfort arrives.

- You feel less alone.

- You are practicing an act of self-care, to which your brain will respond positively.

- You are already changing unhelpful old patterns, neuropathways (circuits), and plasticity (flexibility) by engaging in a new behavior.

I find this incredible, that even in this first minute something quite amazing begins to happen. One simple minute of leaning toward oneself and checking in starts a process of calm, whereby changes in the brain occur and a new sense of perspective can emerge.

What happens in the minutes that follow simply enhances, consolidates, and strengthens this life-changing solution. But before moving on to the next stage of this ten-minute workout, we will practice what has just been covered. So let's go through the first two steps again:

### Take a Moment . . .

Repeat Steps 1 and 2.

Stop what you are doing just now. Put the book down. Make yourself comfortable, close your eyes if that helps, and just acknowledge that your commitment for the next minute is as follows:

- Checking in on how you are today—how are you feeling? Making no judgment. No right, wrong, good or bad. What's going on for you right now?

- Whatever emotions come up, simply acknowledge them and accept them as part of your humanity, with something to teach you. Not trying to change, get rid of, push down, or find more evidence to support the feelings.

Take a few notes on what you notice here—and I suggest that, when possible, you take time out to practice this part of the technique. This could be once a day or a few times a day in the beginning. Just until you feel comfortable with it and that you've really "got it."

# CHAPTER 5:

# Minutes 2 and 3—
# Time for Your Calm Space

Sometimes we just need to get away from it all. I am sure you have all heard that expression. This part of the workout is exactly about doing that: getting away from it all and getting our minds to a calmer place. Realistically, we know that hopping on a cruise ship or catching the next flight to the Bahamas may not be an option, but there are other ways in which we can quickly access a place in our imagination that immediately settles the mind. I often use this technique if I am feeling overwhelmed with demands in my life, whether personally or professionally. I can bring my mind to my Zen, or calm, space—a lake in New England—and suddenly I am more at ease and clarity emerges.

# Step 3: Arriving at Your Calm Space

Now you have managed to complete Steps 1 and 2:

1. Stopping

2. Checking in

Your next stage is to find the Zen-like, or calm, space in your mind.

As I mentioned earlier, I use a technique called tapping, technically called bilateral stimulation, which is used in a therapy called eye movement desensitization and reprocessing (EMDR) and is often referred to as the "safe place" exercise. I hope you won't be put off by the technical term, and simply realize how effectively it works. We are only using EMDR here only as a grounding technique that quickly calms the mind. Once practiced and mastered, you will use it for two minutes in your daily mind workout, after you stop and check in.

I am going to refer to this stage of the workout as going to the *calm space* in our minds. When this technique is used with tapping, it helps someone feel grounded and secure even if they are dealing with difficult emotions or memories.

The amazing aspect of this technique is that it can allow the brain to arrive at a place of calm and stillness quickly by using three installation stages:

1. **Visualization**: Creating an image of a calm, Zen-like space

**2. Language:** Identifying a name for your calm space

**3. Tapping:** See below

For Ten to Zen, we are going to use tapping by means of a simple, *slow*, left- to right-hand alternate rhythmic tapping, either on the thighs or on the upper arms by crossing the arms (like a hug), as shown in the illustration below.

I can imagine you are now wondering what the point of this is. In summary, we know from research that tapping does the following:

1. It creates a relaxation effect.

2. Your thoughts become less stuck.

3. You create some mental distance and are able to stand back from your problems.

4. Your worries decrease.

How exactly tapping causes this to happen is open to some debate and is the subject of much research in the world of neuroscience. One school of thought is that the physiological stimulus created by tapping acts as a diversion that can help create new positive responses within the brain. All we need to know for the purposes of Ten to Zen is that it works. In essence, in creating our calm space by using an image and word alongside the tapping, we send a message to the brain to "install" the positive, calming image, which in turn induces a calmer emotional state and more relaxed body sensations. Every time you close your eyes, go to your calm space, and use the tapping, the installation of your calm place is activated.

**A note of caution:** The tapping aspect of this technique should not be used by anyone with hypersensitivity to sensory stimuli, for example neurological issues, brain injury, migraines, fitting, complex posttraumatic stress disorder (PTSD), or by anyone diagnosed with a dissociative identity disorder. If you are in any doubt or need guidance, please speak to a trained EMDR therapist. Likewise, if any aspect of this particular technique is uncomfortable for you or evokes distress (though I stress that this is very rare), then it can be replaced with an alternative that is comfortable for you, such as simply breathing deeply. That said, for the vast majority of people, this is a safe, effective technique that brings about an instant soothing effect.

# Installing Your Calm Space

This technique requires practice, but once learned it is an incredibly useful and quick way to bring the activity of the mind down a few notches. The idea is that your calm place is mentally "installed" and, after a few practice attempts, you can arrive at this place instantly during your daily workout. Let me reassure you once again that this is a simple, safe, and effective technique.

## Visualizing Your Calm Space

Take a few moments now to identify in your mind an image of a place that represents peace, calm, and relaxation. It can be real or imagined. Common choices are beaches, mountains, countryside, and lakes, but the choice is all yours. The important thing is that it is unique to you and becomes your space, your place to escape and seek solitude. Take a bit of time to think about this, as it will be a place you will visit daily within your Ten to Zen workout. The same place will be used every time you practice Ten to Zen, as the familiarity will help enhance a sense of ease and calm.

Once you have identified your calm space, close your eyes and sit in stillness within this place, noticing what you see and feel—the colors, smells, sensations, and sounds. Let this absorb you for a moment and simply enjoy the sense of escape and freedom that it may bring. This is your time, your space. This is a place of safety, a place of calm, a place of peace.

When you have enjoyed a few moments here, notice where you feel any warm sensations or feelings in your body. Now simply breathe into these sensations and feelings. Slowly enjoy the sense of ease and calm you are feeling and then gently open your eyes again.

 ### Take a Moment . . .

Make a note of your choice of calm space and any sounds, smells, sensations, and so on that accompany it. How does it feel in your body when you allow your mind to go to that place?

## Name Your Calm Space

Now you have identified your calm space and have experienced the stillness of going there, I invite you to choose a word or name for your space. The important thing is that the associative word is unique to you and helps you visualize it in your mind quickly. For example, my space is a lake in New England called Sebago Lake. My word is "serenity." Choose your word and I suggest you write it down now.

**Take a Moment . . .**

Write down your chosen word or name for your space:

Close your eyes again and, as you visualize sitting in your place of calm, repeat the chosen name or word five times in your mind. Allow this image and word to be installed in your mind so that each time you practice Ten to Zen, your mind will automatically access this place. Once installed, after a few practice attempts, you will need to say the name only once in your daily workout and you'll be there.

## Tapping It In

The final stage of installing your calm space is to repeat all the above, but now with the addition of tapping.

1. Close your eyes.

2. Go to your calm space.

3. Say in your mind your word or name.

4. Now, as you arrive in your calm space and with your word in mind, begin the process of tapping to finalize installing your calm space in your brain.

Simply with the image of your calm space and your word in mind, nothing else, start tapping. Do twenty taps in total—

alternate left to right, with *slow* taps on either your thighs or upper arms. (You can use crossed arms for upper arms.) Remember, you are not tapping with both hands at the same time, it is one at a time. Think of it like playing the drums, with alternate taps, left to right, and remember, do this very slowly, at about the speed of a slow handclap.

Each time you arrive at this stage of your workout it will look like this:

- You've done the stopping and checking-in stages.

- You've arrived at your calm space:
    1. Eyes remain closed.
    2. Go to the calm space in your mind (using visualization).
    3. Use your chosen word or name.
    4. Use tapping to finalize installation with twenty taps.

Welcome to your calm space. Next, breathing normally, simply allow yourself to be present in this space in your mind for two minutes, or however long is best for you, somewhat like taking a moment out to sit on the grass on a sunny day. And remember, this is a place you can escape to at any time of the day—or night—when you feel the need to be grounded or to allow your mind to rest. The steps you take to get here in visualizing, naming and tapping mean that you instantly create a Zen-like, calm state of mind, that will help your brain function in a more helpful way.

During this stage of your mental workout the following changes will be happening within your body. We know this from research and neuroscience:

- Your brain activity will be slowing down.

- Your threat center (amygdala) will experience further deactivation.

- Your parasympathetic nervous system will be activated, helping release feel-good hormones such as dopamine and serotonin.

- Greater feelings of calm and stillness will begin to emerge.

- Your breathing and heart rate will slow down.

## Take a Moment . . .

Practice now putting the three components of arriving at your calm space together. With your eyes closed, use your *visualization*, *word*, and *tapping* techniques as described above.

To arrive in the calm space, bring the image of your place to mind, use your chosen word, and do twenty alternate tapping actions. Sit in this place of peace, enjoying the stillness for two minutes. The only goal here is to sit in stillness and allow whatever happens to happen. Think of it as a place to chill and do nothing, allowing the mind to rest and everything else to slow down.

Now, whenever you are ready, try Steps 1, 2, and 3 together:

Step 1. Stopping

Step 2. Checking in

Step 3. Arriving in your calm space

Make a few notes here of how you feel after putting these steps together:

You have now completed your first three minutes of Ten to Zen. Congratulations on getting this far and I hope that, even in these early stages, you are beginning to sample the benefits of what even just three minutes can do for you.

In the next chapter we move to minutes 4 and 5 of your workout, where you will use the breath to deepen your workout even further.

# CHAPTER 6:

# Minutes 4 and 5—
# Time to Breathe

Samuel is an eighteen-year-old man who came to see me for help with his panic attacks. When treating panic attacks it is common practice to teach breathing techniques that help slow down the mind and body. However, in Samuel's case, focusing on his breath made his anxiety worse, as he worried he would stop breathing. Essentially, even his breath was a threat to him. As with most panic-attack cases I see, Samuel was caught in a loop of negative thoughts about his panic-attack symptoms.

One day, I asked him whether he had ever actually stopped breathing when focusing on slowing down his breath or having a panic attack. He paused and smiled, replying, "Of course not." In that moment, something magical happened. Suddenly he was able to see things differently. Rather than see his breath as a threat, we formulated how he could think of it as a source of power and strength; that's what made all the difference to him. Samuel then started to use his breath to calm himself down and simultaneously change how he interpreted his other panic-attack symptoms.

Each breath we take with focused awareness can be a powerhouse of strength and renewal, especially when we are feeling stressed. In my eyes, the breath supports the mind just as nutrients support the body. In this chapter we will explore the power of the breath.

# Step 4: Bringing Breath into Your Workout

You are now familiar with the first three minutes of your Ten to Zen workout, and have practiced slowing down the mind's activity. In this chapter we focus on the next two minutes to further assist the process of quieting down some of the unnecessary activity in your mind. You have now done the following:

1. Stopped

2. Checked in

3. Arrived in your calm space

The next stage is to make use of one of the most grounding and calming tools we have available to us—*our breath*.

## Getting Back in the Driver's Seat

The breath is something we have access to twenty-four hours a day, every moment we are alive on this planet. Connecting to and focusing on our breath is one of the most amazing, simple, and life-affirming means of anchoring ourselves in the present moment.

Focus on the breath is a central aspect of mindfulness, a well-known meditation technique influenced by Buddhist traditions and teachings. As I mentioned earlier, research has produced some hugely encouraging findings on mindfulness's positive impact on the brain. Training the brain to stay focused on one single aspect in the moment, such as breathing, reduces some of the chaotic activity in the mind and helps promote a sense of calm. Essentially, attention is diverted from the busy activity of the mind and redirected to a different focus. Another way of thinking about this is that when we are focusing on the breath, we give the brain another job to do; it likes to be kept busy with a purpose. However, the difference is that now you are in the driver's seat and can start to navigate toward a calmer destination.

Next time you see a baby, observe their breathing. They breathe from their belly, not caring how it looks, with no attempts at holding it in. They breathe in a connected and contented way. Of course, when they need something, they make use of their breath even more by communicating through screams or cries. Their breath is free, not yet restricted by life and its demands.

On the other hand, observe your own breath or that of someone you know. Do it now if you can.

**Take a Moment . . .**

Are you breathing slowly and in a way that is connected to your tummy, or are you breathing shallowly from your chest?

A helpful way to discern this is simply to place your hand on where you feel the rise and fall of the breath. Again, there is no judgment, no right or wrong here, simply notice.

## Connecting to the Breath and Body

Most of the time we are unaware of, and disconnected from, our breath. We breathe in a shallow manner from our chests or our throats, often too quickly, while we are heavily engaged in all the activity in our minds. This becomes exaggerated when our stress levels are raised and we tend to breathe faster. Yet connecting to the breath can be one of the most liberating ways of slowing down our minds, relaxing our bodies, and creating a sense of immediate ease.

I deliberately didn't introduce breath work at the start of your ten minutes, as I believe that the decision first to stop, check in, and get to a calm space in your mind helps utilize the true value of the breath more effectively.

Often, as a therapist, I have said to distressed patients, "Just take a breath," but it hasn't always had the effect I hoped for. I don't think there is anything wrong with the suggestion and in many situations it is effective, but for Ten to Zen I want to maximize this opportunity to use the breath. I have learned from experience that turning down the volume of the mind and getting grounded *before* we turn to the breath can be much more effective and helpful.

These two minutes of breath work are twofold in their focus:

- The first minute simply uses slow, rhythmic, mindful breath to connect to the present moment, with no agenda other than consciously focusing on your breath. Simply watching and observing your breath, the in-breath and the out-breath, then the next in-breath and the next out-breath.

- The second minute uses breath to connect to the body and simply let it be. Again, we know from research that a physically relaxed body has an indirect effect on the mind. Noticing what is going on in the physical body and simply breathing into it can have a remarkably helpful impact.

In fact, fascinating work has been done by psychologists and leading figures in mindfulness worldwide on how breath work can be helpful in relieving pain and other symptoms. Some studies report that the benefits of mindful breathing for pain relief are as favorable as certain pharmacological methods.

# Breath as a Source of Power

I suggest you now add another element into these two minutes of connecting to your breath and body. As you observe it, visualize your breath as a source of power. This power can be used to recharge, re-energize, and strengthen. Each breath you connect to with awareness can become a powerful mechanism for change, just like it was for Samuel.

Think about it—there really is no greater source of power than the breath. It is at the heart of our existence. Without breath we do not exist. However you decide to visualize your breath is your individual choice. You may decide not to use anything and simply observe it, and that is equally fine.

Here are some suggestions that may resonate with you:

- **Topping up the tank.** Using this method, the connection to breath is visualized as akin to topping up the tank of a car, or other vehicle, with fuel. The breath is linked with this image to activate a sense of energy, power, and recharging each time there is connected focus on the breath.

- **Connecting to a higher power.** For people with spiritual beliefs, connecting with the breath can be visualized as linking in with a source of spiritual strength. Each breath that is taken is a breath of renewal and strength, leading to change.

- **Connecting to the universe.** For some, connecting to the universe with each breath may be a useful visual image that activates a sense of energy, connection, and power.

- **Connecting to nature.** Many people find great healing and strength in nature, whether water, mountain, sea, or even a tree. If a particular image helps enhance a sense of renewal and re-energizing, then that could also be used. For example, using the sea with each breath can be visualized as a refreshing and cleansing mechanism.

- **Connecting to science.** This is simply connecting to the breath with knowledge from the world of neuroscience that each breath we observe in a fully connected way contributes to changing our brains in a positive way.

After completing Steps 1, 2 and 3, now add Step 4, connecting to your breath, to your workout.

## Connecting to Your Breath

Focusing on your breathing is broken into two parts, each taking a minute.

### First Minute

With eyes closed and remaining in your Zen-like, calm space, simply observe first how you are breathing by observing your in-breath and your out-breath for a few breaths.

After this, consciously breathe in a rhythmic manner for a count of four seconds, slowly, then breathe out for a count of four seconds, slowly. Repeat this for approximately one minute. (Although you don't need to get too hung up on timings here, this will probably be about eight rounds.) Notice if you become distracted by thoughts or anything else during this focused breathing, and if so, simply acknowledge the distraction and return to focus on the breath.

As with everything in the workout, this doesn't need to be perfect. If you do become distracted by anything, it is the noticing this that shows you are aware and in the present moment. Try not to be hard on yourself; rather, make a decision to be kind and patient. Whatever happens is fine. The magic is purely in noticing whatever is happening for you in that moment.

I suggest you practice this minute of breath work now. If for any reason focusing on your breath is a challenge, you can decide to focus on something else, like a sound or a body sensation. However, I would encourage breath as a first option.

So how did you feel doing that? (Writing down a few thoughts here on your experience may be useful to refer back to.)

## Second Minute

Again with eyes remaining closed, keep focusing on your breath but now allow it to follow its natural flow. During this next minute you are observing your body while breathing and simply noticing whatever you find there. I suggest you observe your body in three sections:

- Your lower body up to your hips
- Your upper body up to your shoulders
- Your head and neck

The only action is to notice and observe what is going on in the body and simply breathe into what you notice. This action will automatically release tension from your body, so allow this to happen without trying too hard to make changes. Let the breath and the power of mindful awareness do the work for you.

Stop for a minute now and try this, as always taking note of any sensations.

## Putting Your Breath Work Together

I now suggest you put minutes 1 and 2 of your breath work together. Just to reiterate:

**For the first minute:** With eyes closed and remaining in your calm space, simply notice how you are breathing by observing your in-breath and out-breath for a few breaths.

After this, consciously breathe in, in a rhythmic manner, for a count of four seconds, slowly, then breathe out for a count of four seconds, slowly. Repeat this for approximately one minute (or about eight rounds). I would suggest you don't worry about specific timing or precision, as you will find your own rhythm and begin to notice the changes.

**For the second minute:** Again with eyes remaining closed, keep focusing on your breath but allow it now to follow its natural flow. During this next minute you are observing your body while breathing and simply noticing whatever you find there. As suggested, observe your body in three parts.

How was this for you?

My key piece of advice as you observe breath and body is aim to make each breath count. There is more power than you can imagine in every breath you take mindfully.

As in previous chapters, I will summarize what the research from neuroscience and psychology tells us about mindful breath and body work, to enable you to understand the value of this part of Ten to Zen:

- On the physiological level, your parasympathetic nerve system is activated, leading to feelings of calmness.

- There is reduction in the activity of the sympathetic nervous system (meaning your stress responses are reduced).

- MRI scans show less activity in the threat center, or amygdala.

- There is improvement in concentration, focus, and creativity.

- Your physical body becomes more relaxed, which in turn positively impacts your mind.

- You will have an improved sense of well-being and happiness.

In the next chapter we will be looking at how we manage thoughts. I suggest you practice the techniques we have covered in this chapter and become familiar and comfortable with them before moving on. Whenever you are ready, try putting all the steps together and remember that this is not a race. Always work at a pace that is comfortable for you.

# CHAPTER 7:

# Minutes 6 and 7—
# Time to Tame Your Thoughts

There is a great story about a woman who goes to therapy because, despite having a very successful life, she can't stop her negative thoughts. The therapist asks her why she thinks she is stuck in negative thought patterns and she responds that she believes she is not good enough. The therapist digs a little deeper, asking why she thinks that is, and she informs the therapist it's because of her impoverished family roots. A few months later the lady is given a Christmas present of a genealogy search and, by tracing her family tree, discovers that she is, in fact, a descendent of royalty, much to her delight. All along there was no concrete evidence to support the belief system that maintained her negative thoughts. Whatever our backgrounds in the real world, it doesn't matter. What really matters is what the woman believed about herself, and what we believe about ourselves.

# You Are Not Your Thoughts

The stories we tell ourselves are often not based on any real facts and say nothing about our value as people. We often do not challenge the negative stories we choose to believe as truth.

So now we will look at ways of managing what for many of us can be a hugely challenging area, our thoughts.

As you may remember from Chapter 3, we know that there is often much random activity that goes on in our brains. We also often have habitual patterns of thought that over time become our "norm." I have so often heard interesting statements such as these:

- "I'm my own worst enemy."

- "I'm a born worrier."

- "Good things don't happen to me."

- "I bring it on myself."

- "I'm not good enough."

Unfortunately, these statements, if repeated often enough, can evolve into real beliefs about ourselves. They become self-fulfilling prophecies.

I once asked a young woman, Sarah, who was dying of cervical cancer at thirty-one, what she meant when she said she wished she had her time again. Her answer made more of an impact on me than she would ever know. She said, "I would spend every day letting go more, and treat myself with a little more kindness."

So I would like you to stop, pause, and think about whether you can identify with Sarah's words.

### Take a Moment . . .

I invite you now to stop and reflect for a few minutes and ask yourself whether you are doing the following:

- Letting go of stuff that doesn't matter

- Using your time wisely

- Treating yourself kindly

Make a few notes here on what answers you find to these questions (remembering there are no right or wrong responses):

Now, in relation to the answers you've given, what changes would you like to make?

# Who Is Running the Show, You or Your Thoughts?

This chapter, describing minutes 6 and 7 of your Ten to Zen workout, will use techniques from the world of cognitive behavioral therapy (CBT). This model of therapy links how our patterns of thought impact how we feel. Our thoughts in turn are maintained by the everyday rules or beliefs that we develop about ourselves, others, and the world. These beliefs are a result of our experiences in the world, which are normally heavily influenced by the core beliefs that have been set in place by our family dynamics, culture, religions, or events that have happened to us. I think a useful way to think of CBT is to imagine a cake with three layers:

- **Top layer: our thoughts**. Those random images, stories, imaginings that go on in our heads, non-stop at times.

- **Middle layer: our beliefs**. Essentially the rules we have for living, which are personal and unique to every one of us. Our belief systems are normally characterized by a series of *should be* or *must be* premises. For example, *I should never say "no." I must be a good person. I must not disappoint others.*

- **Bottom layer: our core beliefs**. The felt sense in the depth of our gut that may cry out with a sense of helplessness or worthlessness and questions our lovability or whether we are good enough.

The amazing aspect of the CBT model is that research demonstrates that when we change how we relate to our thoughts, it has a positive impact on both our beliefs and our core beliefs. In essence, what goes on in the top layer of the cake seeps down in a drizzle fashion into the middle and bottom layers of the cake. If thought patterns are continuously negative or critical, then this will filter down and reinforce both our negative belief and our core beliefs. On the other hand, if thought patterns become more adaptive (or flexible), then they impact our beliefs in a more helpful way. You may have noticed that I avoided using the term "positive thinking" and that choice is deliberate. I am not a fan of positive thinking as a concept. I'll explain why.

## What's Wrong with Positive Thinking?

I prefer to use the term "adaptive thinking" because I think it leads to more realistic, constructive changes. There is no sugarcoating the fact that sometimes life is tough. There are times in life when "positive thinking" about an event or life is simply not possible. If someone has experienced a horrific loss or bereavement, then thinking "positively" about it may seem crude or insensitive. "Look on the bright side" just isn't going to cut it. In my time working with the dying, I frequently heard people, including professionals, trying to use positive platitudes in situations that were not going to have a happy ending. Encouragement of unrealistic positive thinking was often unhelpful, leaving the patient feeling like they had failed for not "beating the cancer" or not "looking on the bright side" enough, whereas encouraging adaptive thinking often worked better. Helping patients to think about living life in the way that made them happiest within the realms of what was possible was more beneficial.

I understand that in desperate circumstances, finding hope is important, but often that hope is found in learning the flexibility to adapt and live fully with what is, rather than entering into magical thinking about what might have been.

In an everyday context, telling someone to think positively and believe that they are the most beautiful, successful, incredible person on the planet may also not cut it; focusing on the true strengths and possibilities that that person has may be a much more helpful approach. We often see this with children who are told from an early age that they will be the next David Beckham or Naomi Campbell. Some of the surveys done with children around future ambition highlight that the majority want to be famous when they grow up. Yet the statistics tell us only a tiny percentage will achieve this. Essentially, what I am highlighting is the importance of keeping things in perspective when it comes to restructuring how we think.

So let's come back to minutes 6 and 7 of your Ten to Zen workout. These next two minutes will be dedicated to identifying unhelpful thinking patterns and knowing what you can let go of. For this to happen, you need to look at the evidence for these thought patterns and examine how you can relate differently to these thoughts.

To illustrate this I will share the example of Jimmy, who struggled with managing stress at work. Jimmy grew up with a very critical father and there was a lot of shouting and arguing at home. His father would regularly threaten Jimmy and tell him he was useless and, as a result, Jimmy underachieved at school. Later, as an adult, he lacked confidence and had a sense that he was "less than" others. He came to me displaying three key challenges around his thoughts:

- **Catastrophizing and thinking the worst.** Each time Jimmy did not meet a work target or deadline, he would immediately tell himself that he would be fired, even though it was common for staff in his company not to reach all their required targets, and he had never been fired for this in his ten years with the company.

- **Self-criticism.** He was highly self-critical of his work and his ability to manage his job.

- **Mind reading.** Jimmy would often misinterpret his manager, assuming he was thinking critically of him.

Jimmy's life experiences resulted in him developing negative thought patterns and beliefs about himself. He assumed that anyone in authority was likely to behave like his father. In fact, there was further factual evidence, which he had never explored or considered, that revealed the following:

- He was in the top 5 percent of performers in his company.

- His boss had never criticized him.

- He was very capable and managed his job well.

Jimmy's stress was maintained by his thoughts and inter-pretation of what was going on, which of course were heavily influenced by his past. In recognizing his thought patterns and understanding them more deeply, he was able to start letting go, and seeing the thoughts for what they were—just thoughts, not facts.

Often it is not the events in our lives that create the great-est challenges for us, but our interpretation of these events. There is great freedom in discovering the patterns that may be active in our minds and learning the key skill of observing them and letting go. Within these two minutes of your daily workout you will deliberately bring to mind your identified, unhelpful thought patterns, with no judgment, and then learn the art of observing them and letting them drift by. To do this it is essential to be able to identify what your patterns are, and it can be quite a shock at first when you realize how prominent and persistent some of them can be. Trust me on this one; I was shell-shocked when I became aware of some of my own patterns.

## Jack-in-the-Box Thoughts

Identifying unhelpful thought patterns should be an interest-ing exercise to complete. While I am aware the content may seem negative or even irritating, my suggestion is that you approach it with a sense of humor and curiosity. It will be like uncovering a part of you that you were never really aware existed, because negative thought patterns are very auto-mated, almost like fish that jump out of water. Assuming you are alive and breathing (unlike the poor fish), you will undoubtedly identify with some of the thought patterns on page 103. I have yet to meet anyone who doesn't.

It always amuses me when I complete this exercise during a Ten to Zen workshop. When I ask for anyone who identifies with the patterns to show their hand, people sheepishly look around as if they are about to be arrested for committing a crime. There is an expression on most faces that reads, "Is there anyone else like me in this room?" Indeed there is—everyone in the room! By the end of the day, almost everyone has both hands in the air when I ask the same question.

The problem with these unhelpful thought patterns is that they are so familiar and readily available that they can feel very normal. Negative, critical thoughts jump up like a jack-in-the-box, often without warning. Really, they should come with a government health warning. Often they come with such power and credibility that we listen to them initially and then work hard to get rid of them, which makes them come back with renewed strength. It is how the mind works. If you try to push something away, the processes of the brain will keep coming back to it until it gets the attention it needs. However the solution to this problem is simple. Stop running away from your thoughts. They won't harm you and they don't define you.

# What Are Your Critical Voices Telling You?

A participant in a Ten to Zen workshop I once delivered was struggling to get in touch with her compassionate self during the workout.

I asked her what her compassionate voice sounded like when she was struggling, and she said, "It's shouting at me, 'Get on with it, you silly woman!'" The group laughed when she added, "And you should hear my critical voice when it gets started!"

I think we can all make a guess at what her critical voice might sound like, and no doubt every reader will have their own unique critic waiting in the wings to pounce at any opportunity.

## Don't Pick the Booby Prizes

When thinking about the critical voice, I like to use an analogy. There is a British game show called *The Generation Game*, in which prizes would be placed on a conveyor belt and the contestant had to remember them in order to win them. There would always be a kettle, a cuddly toy, and a set of suitcases. I think our minds can be a little like that conveyer belt, with a few old favorites always showing up— self-criticism, self-judgment, and self-deprecation.

Unlike the prizes on the game show, the prizes on the conveyor belt of the mind are booby prizes. We are all guilty of harsh treatment of self, and within your daily ten minutes you'll be working towards moving away from this and show-ing yourself confidence and belief, knowing you deserve more. A calmer mind in itself isn't enough because the mind will never always be calm, and life will never always be smooth. How we respond to ourselves when the storms of the mind or life move in is more pertinent.

Within your ten minutes you will bravely face your thought patterns, paying particular attention to the ones that create the biggest challenges. This will vary from day to day, but the key is to be able to identify what is going on for you so that in time you can almost jokingly say, "Oh, here is my critical judge again." The thought patterns become like old friends that we can begin to take less seriously when they start their banter. Again, they are not your enemies. They simply need you to acknowledge them. Your goal is to develop the skill of acknowledging and letting them go. This is key. Essentially, it is about relating to your thoughts mindfully.

## The Usual Suspects

I will now name the six key thought-pattern offenders that in my experience create the most difficulties for people. You may have others, so don't be afraid to add them to the list. I have given these thought patterns character names, because that's what they are. Just like characters in a play, they sometimes take to the stage. So here are some of the lead characters of the unhelpful mind:

## The Critical Judge

Judgmental, critical thinking is exhausting because self-blame is relentless. The tone of this thought pattern is harsh, presenting you with evidence that it's all your fault, you should have known better, how could you let this happen? It is normally not a fair judge; in fact, quite the opposite with very biased views all pointing back at one guilty party: you. Typical thought patterns could be these:

- You never get it right.

- How could you do this?

- I told you this would happen—this is typical you.

- You never learn.

- You're useless, pathetic, and weak.

## The Military General

Regimented thinking is the order of the day with the Military General's thought patterns, which feature *should* and *must* as a priority. There are lots of rules about how you should behave and what you must do to prove yourself worthy, likeable, lovable; the list is endless. There is little room for flexible thinking here. The tone is harsh, lacking in empathy, and demanding—you must stand to attention to its demands. Typical thought patterns could be these:

- You must please people or they will reject you.

- You should be a good person.

- You should think of others first.

- You must be successful and must not fail.

- You should not expect too much.

## The Dramatist

High-energy, dramatic, catastrophic thinking comes out to play when the Dramatist shows up. Little evidence is weighed up and rational thinking takes a back seat. Everything is a disaster; it's all going wrong. Someone better wipe your brow quickly, as you fear you may collapse under all the strain. Typical thought patterns could be these:

- You won't cope.

- This is all too much.

- It's going to be a complete disaster.

- This is all going to go wrong.

- It's all ruined now.

## The Psychic

Conclusions are reached quickly when this thought pattern arises and one plus one suddenly equals twenty-three. The odd expression on your manager's face at the meeting tells you that he thinks you are bad at your job. The "look" from the girlfriend or boyfriend, husband or wife is enough to let you know they are about to end it. Typical thought patterns could be these:

- What did that look mean?

- They think I'm useless.

- I know this is all going wrong.

- That person ignoring me must mean something.

- What's the point?

## The Trash Collector

Anything constructive, helpful, or useful is immediately disposed of when this thought pattern arrives. Nothing good happens for you. Why should you expect good things to happen? You don't deserve anything good in your life. This voice will advise you to focus on all the negative stuff, and dispose of anything else. Typical thought patterns could be these:

- Don't waste your time.

- It will never work out.

- Yes, I know, but . . .

- I don't deserve this.

- Good things never happen to me.

## The Terminator

"Merciless" is the only description for this thought pattern when it makes its debut in your mind. There is little thinking to be done here, as the conclusions have already been reached, telling you that you are any of the following: stupid, useless, worthless, dirty, bad, ugly. Its tone is harsh and cruel and leaves you feeling invalidated and destroyed. Typical thought patterns could be these:

- I am disgusting.

- I am worthless.

- I am stupid and a loser.

- Who would want me?

- I am a failure.

Do any of these sound familiar?

Now let me ask you a simple question:

Read back over some of these unhelpful thinking styles and ask yourself, would you speak to someone you care about in this way? Would you tell them they won't cope, they are useless, ugly, a failure and don't deserve anything good to happen to them?

Your answer to this is likely to be "no," so let me present a second question:

If you wouldn't speak to someone you care about in that way, why would you engage in and believe thoughts that tell you this about yourself?

Sometimes the stories that our minds tell us can be nothing short of cruel and unkind. In learning to take a step back from them, you begin the process of relating to yourself and your thoughts in a kinder, more compassionate way. Remember, thought patterns are habitual and often there is little evidence to support any of them as true. You are not your thoughts. How you relate to your thoughts will truly change how you live.

Within Ten to Zen we greet thoughts as guests and dedicate time for them. Thoughts, instead of becoming the enemy, become something we are curious and friendly about. They are no longer hidden, pushed down, battled with. They become part of our experience, things that we know will come and go just like the clouds in the sky. In time you will come to know that no matter what is going on in your mind, behind the clouds there is always a blue sky.

 **Take a Moment . . .**

### Tracking Your Thoughts

First, make a list of any of the thought patterns on pages 113–116 that you can identify with, and write down the thoughts you are having as they emerge. If you have other thought patterns I have not included that you would like to add a character name to, please do.

Second, whatever your key patterns are, take some time now to examine what evidence you have to support these thoughts as being true. For example, do you have a strong Critical Judge thought pattern telling you that everything is your fault? Where exactly is the evidence for that? Is there a possibility that this isn't true and is in fact false? What would an alternative thought look like?

List each thought pattern that you identified earlier, and then list the "evidence" that shows if these thoughts are true or false.

To give you an example:

**Critical Judge thought:** "Everything bad that happens in my life is totally my fault."

**Evidence for this being true:** "I can't find any real evidence for this being all my fault. Some unfortunate things happened but I didn't cause them."

**Evidence for this being false:** "I didn't choose any of these bad things to happen. And, in fact, I always do my best to stop them."

**Alternative thought:** "Some bad things have happened in my life that are not my responsibility."

# Step 5: Observing Your Thoughts within Your Ten to Zen Workout

So far in this chapter we've helped you create some space between you and your thoughts, in order to help identify any problematic patterns you are stuck in. It is essential to identify these patterns before embarking on this next part of your daily Ten to Zen.

Within your Ten to Zen daily workout I suggest you complete minutes 6 and 7 with your eyes closed and structured as I describe here, in two stages of approximately one minute each:

## 1. First Minute

Deliberately bring to mind your challenging thought patterns and welcome them in, almost like guests. As you now have explored the evidence to discount many of these patterns, you will know instinctively what to let go of. I know it sounds like an odd suggestion to do this, but in bringing unhelpful thought patterns into present-moment awareness, you will discharge some of their power. If your thought patterns start to play out the familiar old themes, then you can make a decision to simply observe, let go, and almost watch them fade away. With the help of your daily Ten to Zen workout, you create a new relationship with your thoughts and they will become less scary and intimidating. Likewise, you are also creating new neuropathways in relation to your negative thought patterns. Essentially, you are moving from maladaptive patterns to more adaptive patterns, courageously facing the bully that can be your mind.

## 2. Second Minute

Simply sit with your thoughts generally and observe them as if you were watching a movie or observing clouds in the sky. Coming and going. Not engaging with them, not thinking them over or trying to change them. Simply observing. The explanation for this is simple. When we observe a busy mind, it is rather like observing a naughty child. When a child becomes aware they are being watched they are less likely to act out, and our minds respond in a similar way. The activity automatically begins to slow and we move out of autopilot to a more present-moment awareness that ultimately brings a sense of stillness.

Practice this work on thoughts a few times if you find it helpful. First, bring your negative thought patterns to your awareness. Second, observe your thoughts generally.

I now encourage you to practice your first seven minutes of Ten to Zen and again take it slowly and at a pace that works for you.

Here's a summary of the steps we've covered so far:

| | |
|---|---|
| Minute 1: Step 1. | Stopping |
| Minute 1: Step 2. | Checking in |
| Minute 2 and 3: Step 3. | Arriving in your calm space |
| Minute 4 and 5: Step 4. | Breathing consciously |
| Minute 6 and 7: Step 5. | Managing your thoughts |

In the next chapter we move on to minutes 8 and 9, and become more mindful.

## CHAPTER 8:

# Minutes 8 and 9—
# Time to Be Mindful

Last year I was invited to present a Ten to Zen workshop for a group of lawyers. Most were very keen to be there, apart from one guy, Tommy. He started the day by saying quite forcefully that he thought mindfulness was a "lot of mumbo jumbo." As you can gather, Tommy wasn't holding back. Respectful of his view but simultaneously curious about the ferocity of his opinions, I calmly asked him what helped him recharge his batteries in the best way.

Instantly he responded that for him, beach vacations in quiet destinations worked perfectly. When I asked him why, his response made me smile: "Because when I'm on the beach, I let go of everything and just enjoy the moment. It's pure heaven."

I thanked him for opening the day with such a clear description of mindfulness.

Tommy looked perplexed but by the end of the day he understood my meaning. He was rather pleased that, unknown to him, he had been practicing mindfulness in his own way all along. Tommy had never considered these as "mindful" moments, but when he described his enjoyment of the sun on his back, feeling the breeze on his face, hearing the waves, and properly tasting a beer because there were no distractions, he was describing living mindfully in those moments.

This may also be true of you, even when drinking your cup of tea. Anything can be practiced mindfully and, yes, it's still a form of meditation! It's not all about crossed-legged chanting with burning incense.

I recognize that these moments Tommy described on vacation are not truly representative of everyday life when it might be cold outside and work deadlines and family pressures are looming. Nonetheless, I believe these moments of letting be and enjoying the present are possible at any point in the day. So the benefits Tommy described are available to us twenty-four hours per day if we choose to allow ourselves to be wholly in the present moment.

Some of you may be wondering what the benefit of this step is. I will explain because, as I said earlier, I believe these techniques work best if you have a firm understanding of why they will be helpful. To help with this, I'm going to share a little of my experience of living mindfully.

# What Is Mindfulness?

First, though, I'd like to explain my understanding of what mindfulness is.

As you may be aware, the roots of mindfulness arise from Buddhist traditions and remain a core aspect of Buddhist teachings. Over the past twenty years, particularly, there has been increasing interest in the practice from the Western world. Neuroscientists and psychologists continue producing fascinating results on the benefits of mindfulness, as I've mentioned a few times.

People like Tommy often express initial concern when I teach mindfulness or Ten to Zen. I've been told they worry that I'm going to arrive in a robe and that's it's going to be a day of bells, chanting, strict breathing, and other "weird stuff." It's not. Such practice within secular groups is totally understandable if that is their way, and is to be respected. However, in everyday life and within your Ten to Zen, the approach is a down-to-earth, relatable means of using these life-changing techniques.

This book is not focused on any particular religious traditions, but I do want to pay homage to the Buddhist community and honour their tireless work in introducing and promoting mindfulness worldwide. Most of the distress we experience on a daily basis is a result of what goes on in our minds, as you now know from Chapter 3: our thoughts, our interpretations of events, our ruminating on the past and obsessing about what the future will bring. Mindfulness encourages awareness of the present moment; whatever you are doing, wherever you are, *without judgment*. This enables you to *let go of the past and not worry about the future*. Within your ten minutes it is necessary to allow such moments, hence the inclusion of these dedicated minutes.

## My Journey to Mindfulness

Throughout my career I have attended dozens of mindfulness events with varying degrees of helpfulness. As it grows in popularity and becomes "sexier," mindfulness can sometimes be presented in a way that is either too complicated or, dare I say it, even a little sanctimonious. I trained to teach mindfulness at Oxford and felt very privileged to be taught by people who lived and embodied the principles of mindful living. However, my initial introduction to the world of mindfulness was quite an odd experience for someone who tends not to hold superstitious views.

One afternoon I was in a bookstore in London, looking at the psychology section, when a book literally dropped from the shelf. The book was called *The Power of Now*. I picked up the book, thought the title was interesting, and that was that. A week later, a friend of mine, a Catholic priest, was travelling to South Africa from Ireland and asked to meet me at Heathrow for coffee. As we were saying our good-byes he produced a book saying, "Oh yeah, I bought this for you, I think you will really like it." Yes, it was the exact same book, *The Power of Now*.

Of course I had to read the book. I was compelled to believe that someone, something, somewhere, was trying to tell me something. This proved to be true. By the end of the book I felt a real sense of liberation. I had never realized I had the power to simply observe some of what goes on in my mind. My life genuinely changed that day, and my curiosity for living mindfully has continued to grow and I live a happier life as result. In addition, some of the most challenging moments of my life have been managed with greater ease as a result of reading that book and living the principles of mindfulness. I learned I could create space between my mind and myself. Equally, I discovered that all things pass; everything passes. True peace and contentment are found in the here and now. This I know to be true.

## Step 6: The Practice

Mindfulness principles run through all the techniques I've used in Ten to Zen, layered with the other specialist psychological therapies I use. Minutes 8 and 9 of your workout are purely dedicated to arriving and sitting in the present moment, using the art of mindfulness to gain strength for the day ahead.

So far you have learned to practice the following:

Step 1.  Stopping

Step 2.  Checking in

Step 3.  Arriving in your calm space

Step 4.  Breathing consciously

Step 5.  Managing your thoughts

These next minutes, with some of the hyperactivity of the mind now settled, are simply about sitting in stillness and noticing.

So now, remain in the same position as you started, with eyes kept closed. Now you have completed your work on thought, it is time to move into mindful stillness.

During these two minutes you have a number of choices in terms of what you decide to focus on, or you may decide simply to be present with wherever your attention goes. My advice would be to stay with a single point of focus to start with. For example, during these minutes you might decide to focus on your breath or body again, or try a new area:

- **Breath:** Observing your in-breath and out-breath. Not trying to change your breath. Simply observing it, wherever you notice it most in your body, for example your nostrils, chest, stomach. In this act of mindfulness, your mind may drift or you may become distracted, but each time your mind drifts, simply return to focus on the breath, without criticism or judgment. I think a helpful way of thinking about this is how we might communicate when training a puppy. Every time we go off track, it's fine: "Come on, boy, come back here." *Even the act of noticing your wandering mind is a return to mindfulness.* The focused awareness is changing your brain.

- **Body:** Observing generally what you notice in your body. No doubt your attention will be directed to certain areas. The premise is identical; you are not aiming to change anything, but simply to observe what is going on in your body—any sensations, discomfort, pain, relaxed areas, or areas of tension. If you do notice any areas of discomfort, then you can simply observe, breathe into that area and then let go. Our physical bodies often hold the score for what is emotionally unexpressed.

- **Sound:** Observing sounds you hear. Allowing the sounds to come and go but not creating stories around the sounds; simply noticing all the sounds around you, the tone, volume, quality of sound, or anything that particularly draws your attention. Again, if distracted by thoughts or anything else, simply return to focus on the sound without judgment or criticism. It is the noticing that is part of mindful awareness.

- **Emotions:** If you do notice a particular emotional state, such as anger, sadness, calm, frustration, and so on, you may decide to allow your awareness to move towards the emotional state and simply stay present with the emotion and breathe normally; not aiming to think through the emotion or change the feeling. Similar to the other areas of focus, it is a simple focused attention on the feeling.

Ultimately the choice of focus is yours and it may vary depending on circumstance. If you are practicing in the garden in summer, you may decide to concentrate on smells. The important thing is making the decision for the minute to focus on one area and stay with that focus. Essentially, you are retraining the brain to focus, helping restore some equilibrium when there is simply too much activity going on.

If you notice your mind wandering off to think about other things or to plan the day during this stage or other stages in your workout, this is totally normal. Each time this happens, simply return your attention back to your point of focus. This is the practice of mindfulness and what will ultimately make all the difference to your life. It's the awareness and noticing that inform you that you are present.

## The Power in This Moment

This part of your practice allows a stillness to emerge. Within the stillness everything is possible. Whatever is going on in your life is brought back to a place of perspective, because the only thing you have is now. I like to view it in several ways:

- I see it as a moment when suddenly light emerges.

- I see it as a moment when the noise stops.

- I see it as a moment when the clouds clear.

- I see it as a moment of connecting to infinite possibilities.

- I see it as a moment when it is possible to connect to the true essence of humanity.

- It is a moment of truth within which the fictional stories we tell ourselves cease.

- It is a moment of being fully alive that will set you up for the rest of the day.

- In this moment you will also consolidate the work you have done in your first seven minutes of practice.

## Why This Will Be Helpful

The answer is simple: it works and everything changes. I can confidently state that every person I have every worked with therapeutically has two things in common: they get stuck in the past or bound by fears of the future and they give themselves a tough time with self-criticism or judgments.

Mindfulness takes another route by advocating two key principles: letting go of the past and the future, and staying in the present moment; in essence, allowing things to be as they are. And no longer beating yourself up, but instead practicing more kindness to and acceptance of self.

## In Mindfulness Practice

* There is no past—it's gone.

* There is the future—it's yet to come.

* The only thing to concentrate on is now.

* Even if we get distracted, we can come back to the present moment.

* Nothing is judged.

* Compassion toward oneself is central.

* The brain is allowed time and space to rest, recover, and recharge.

* The single point of focus during mindfulness retrains the brain to become less busy; essentially it is given a new focus—to be present.

Think back to Tommy's description on page 122. When he is on the beach he is present with his experiences and having a mindfulness moment. He has his moment of "heaven."

# Experiencing Life in the Moment

Mindfulness is the simplest yet most powerful option available to us as humans. We can choose at any point to be mindful—eating, walking, running, playing with the children—we simply make a decision to be fully present and become aware of the one area of focus in that moment. If the mind distracts us, we return to focus. We step out of autopilot and experience what is happening, rather than feel like we are on a treadmill. We are alive, rather than just existing.

Let me ask you to consider a few questions:

* When was the last time you truly tasted the food you ate?

* When were you last truly present with someone in a conversation?

* When did you last walk, aware of the sensation of walking?

* When did you last truly experience a hot shower, feeling the water, enjoying the heat, or smelling the scent of the shower gel?

Whatever your answers to this, I encourage you to consider how much of life you are truly experiencing. Or does it feel like you "go through the motions" every day?

This minute of mindful practice is a reminder to wake up for the remainder of your day. It is your call to becoming aware:

- To live, rather than exist

- To flourish, rather than just survive

- To be fully awake to the wonder and possibilities of each moment, whatever they might be

## The Evidence

When we decide to pay attention to what is going on in the present moment without judgment, some incredible changes happen over a period of time, as informed by research evidence:

- MRI scans show that people who practice mindfulness for even ten minutes per day have healthier brain scans, with less activity in their stress areas, more plasticity (flexibility), and even changes in gray matter.

- Health, well-being, and sleep all improve.

- Concentration, memory, and mood all improve.

- Anxiety decreases.

- Everyday functioning improves.

- Health and pain issues improve.

- Athletes perform better.

- Students achieve better results.

- Workplaces report increased performance.

The message is clear. I believe these results can be attributed to two key factors beyond what goes on physiologically. Firstly, we return to simplicity in mindfulness within a world that is often frenzied. Secondly, we stop judging our experiences—whatever is present in mindfulness is embraced and accepted, even the tough stuff. The battleground of the mind ceases momentarily, and then increasingly, with practice.

## The Mindful Wisdom of the Dying

I want to close this chapter by paying tribute to those who truly taught me the value of living mindfully in the moment: those many people who allowed me to journey with them while dying.

Each dying person I have been privileged to work with has reminded me that each breath we have is a gift; that every sound, smell, sunrise should never be taken for granted. Each moment is a new start with much to offer. The decision to pay attention is pivotal.

One day I sat with a young man in his late twenties, Lucas, who was dying of leukemia. He was planning one last trip away with his friends to Amsterdam, and, as you can imagine, the conversation was entertaining. Then during our chat, I noticed the tone of the conversation changing. His attention waned as he looked out the window, staring intently at the sky. When his attention eventually returned to the room he looked a little tearful.

After a moment of silence, Lucas commented that he had never before noticed how often the sky changes. To be honest, I initially wondered whether his medication was causing him to hallucinate, but when he spoke a bit more it was clear to me then he was lucid and fully aware.

He explained that every moment was like a new painting appearing in the sky. Each movement of cloud or each change of color delivered something fresh and new. I was astounded by the wonder in his eyes and the excitement in his voice as he described this. It was as if he was noticing the sky with its changing landscape for the first time. In that moment he was truly present, appreciative of the moment, and seeing the world with childlike eyes, full of wonder and curiosity.

Sometimes now when I look at a changing sky, I think of him. I wonder whether Lucas ever knew how much he influenced me. I am reminded of the great wonder and gift of every changing moment. It keeps me curious and interested, not just in the changing sky, but in the new possibilities in every moment. These possibilities are available to you in these ten minutes every day. There are opportunities within each moment of your ten-minute workout, within each moment of your day. The choice is all yours.

A dying person often expresses with great wisdom the lessons to be found in living fully in the present moment. They learn that all we truly have is now. The past has gone.

The future is not yet here. Everything is to be found in the here and now. Each moment is to be lived.

*We are all dying.* Difficult to think about, I know, but true. Buddhists teach us of the value in reminding ourselves of our mortality, as within that can emerge a sense of freedom and perspective. Our moment, too, will come to pass to the next stage, whatever your beliefs. Yet we are all also alive. There is so much to be experienced in the meantime in the living. It's about making our lives count. Earlier I joked about the epitaph on our tombstones reading, "Completely deranged, but had lovely teeth." How would you like yours to read? It is worth pondering, I think.

Within all this uncertainty and the ever-present knowledge that we, too, will die, there is sometimes distress. We grapple with trying to hold on to control, but that is pointless. Making that decision to let go and allow things to be is the beginning of a newfound freedom. There is no day but today, no moment but now, and perhaps that is enough.

Within your workout and particularly during your minutes of mindfulness, I encourage you to bear in mind some of the lessons I share with you from the dying. I encourage you not to view this as bleak, but as liberating. A route to perhaps taking life less seriously. In taking that moment in stillness, we arrive at a new state of awareness, celebrating the power of the present moment with fresh eyes. It then has a domino effect on the rest of the day, the rest of the week, the rest of our lives.

A minute of stillness can open the door to a lifetime of change.

## Putting It All Together

Now take time to practice these two minutes of mindfulness. When you become comfortable with this, you can add them on to the rest of the mind workout:

Step 1.  Stopping

Step 2.  Checking in

Step 3.  Arriving in your calm space

Step 4.  Breathing consciously

Step 5.  Managing your thoughts

Step 6.  Being in the present moment

The final minute, minute 10, covered in the next chapter, involves mentally putting on your Ten to Zen "cloak," which embodies my core Ten to Zen principles for living. These principles have been woven in with the techniques throughout the book as a way of living.

# CHAPTER 9:

# Minute 10— Time to Embody Your Ten to Zen Principles

A while ago I started working with an actor I'll call Charlie. Despite being very well known and successful in his career, he suffered from severe stage fright. Charlie had suffered anxiety symptoms since childhood, and even though we could make sense of his negative thought patterns, none of the usual anxiety-reducing techniques worked. One session, I noticed Charlie talked a lot about how costumes impacted the way he portrayed a character. When I asked him which costume he preferred, he immediately referred to a velvet cloak that had made him feel upright, stable, and calm while he was playing a Shakespeare character in London's West End. I sensed that we had our solution.

Before attempting any of the techniques we worked on, I started to show Charlie how he could mentally "put on" an imaginary velvet cloak before every show, to help him feel the stability and calm he needed to perform. Remarkably, it worked brilliantly, and since then I have used the technique on countless people very successfully.

As a result of this I developed the idea of a "mental cloak" for the closing section of Ten to Zen. This "mental cloak" embodies three Ten to Zen "principles for living": acceptance, compassion, and authenticity. I will explain more.

So when the everyday flow of our life becomes daunting, like Charlie, we can learn to mentally put on a "cloak" that represents certain principles. A cloak is warm, protective, and heavy and can help us stand tall, ready to face whatever comes along. It can add a sense of gravitas, confidence, and stature and allow us to take our place on the stage of life with greater comfort and ease.

Within the context of Ten to Zen the purpose of this "mental cloak" is similar to the way in which Charlie used it. Like any cloak, it can be fitted to suit you, and you can—should you wish—envisage the color, material, and style that will enable you to stand tall.

## The Principles of Your Ten to Zen Cloak

I call this imaginary armor a cloak, but you can call it anything you want to. The principles weaved into the fabric of this cloak are there to help you feel supported and safe throughout your day. Mentally donning this cloak will help you connect to your own strength, wisdom, and kindness and allow the best version of you to manage your day. It will be like your personal armor, giving you an extra layer of protection.

Each day, in the final minute of your workout you will visualize mentally putting on this cloak and focus on three key principles that embody the essence of this workout:

- **Acceptance**

- **Compassion**

- **Authenticity**

Alongside this visualization, I encourage you to create something that you can keep with you at all times that will act as a reminder of these principles, something you can take out and look at in the final minute of Ten to Zen. For example, I carry with me a small laminated card with the three principles and their key meanings for me. It reminds me of the choices I make in terms of how I live my life.

Today I choose:

- **Compassion:** to myself, to all I meet, and particularly to those I struggle with

- **Acceptance:** it is what it is; this, too, will become a memory

- **Authenticity:** I aim simply to try to be the best version of me, and when I can't, I try again

## Adding on the Final Layer

Ultimately the techniques within the ten minutes are not, in themselves, the complete package. While they act quickly and in a very effective manner to enable you to feel calmer, if they are accompanied by these principles for living, they will do much more than just provide calmer moments. Weaving these principles into your workout will take it to another level. They will act as your wise voice, your supportive voice of wisdom, always available at your side.

## Step 7: Being Your Authentic Self

Have you ever listened to someone deliver a talk that doesn't make you feel anything? I recently observed a young woman deliver a presentation for a local homelessness organization. She was articulate and professional and delivered all the information, but it was clear she had no real passion for the subject. I found out later she was pursuing other career options, which of course was fine, but I was intrigued by how that translated in the room.

A few weeks later I listened to the same presentation delivered by a middle-aged man. He was a service user from the organization and had himself formerly been homeless. His passion, interest, and enthusiasm for the subject were tangible and people stopped to listen. He engaged and held his audience. The difference was that he was compassionate to the needs of the homeless, his authenticity was obvious, and his acceptance of, and clarity on, their needs was unquestionable. His heart was in it and his passion was palpable.

This is relevant to you because it is important that the commitment you make to your Ten to Zen workout has passion and authenticity. If you approach your workout with the same principles and passion as the middle-aged man, everything can change. Anyone can effectively use the techniques, but making the commitment to embody the principles involves digging deeper.

This is more than just feeling calmer or less stressed. It is ultimately about changing how you relate to yourself. If you just go through the motions, using all the techniques without acceptance, compassion, and authenticity, then there is a risk that's all it becomes—just going through the motions.

When I was working with the dying, I heard from countless people who regretted treating themselves harshly, and not living authentically, or not being completely true to themselves. So what I offer in these three principles for living are my insights as a human being and a professional who has witnessed much suffering. I believe that living with acceptance, compassion, and authenticity can relieve this suffering immeasurably.

# Acceptance

I'm sure most of you are familiar with the classic Beatles song "Let It Be." I can remember as a young boy finding comfort in the lyrics, which reminded me I had permission to let things go, to let them be. As I grew up, letting go and allowing things to be became a much bigger challenge. An anxious mind has little tolerance for uncertainty, so letting go isn't easy. But I also learned that holding on with a need to be in control inadvertently created more worry.

We learn to meet negative emotions as a threat and avoid them at all costs, and it's the same with negative experiences. We tend to get caught in similar patterns of not wanting them to be:

- Why me?

- Not again

- I can't believe this is happening

- This is just my luck

- I am doomed

- I knew it was too good to be true

 **Take a Moment . . .**

Stop for a moment now and consider a recent minor irritation. For example, a delay that meant missing a bus or getting stuck in a traffic jam. I want you to consider how you managed that situation and which approach you are more familiar with:

A.  This is what it is. It's a little frustrating but out of my control. There is nothing I can do about it for now. I will catch up on a phone call or listen to some music. It will all work out.

B.  I don't believe this is happening. That's my day ruined now. Why does this always happen to me? I might as well cancel all my plans.

There is no judgment of whatever your response was. It may have been a clear-cut A or B response, or a mixture of both, but I would like you to consider the following:

Which response do you think leads to an increase in distress, an increase in blood pressure, an increase in your stress responses, and a negative impact on other circumstances in the day?

The answer, of course, is B. Now consider whether that's because of the circumstances or because of your response to the circumstances.

Circumstances are what they are—they are often out of your control. Yes, sometimes you can explore viable alternatives that can be helpful. However your response to the circumstances and a willingness to *accept what is* in the moment can potentially make all the difference to the experience for you.

## Acceptance Doesn't Mean Defeat

Perhaps some of you are questioning whether acceptance is really a helpful concept or not. A patient recently asked me whether acceptance meant admitting defeat or failure. It's a valid question.

In my eyes, it is neither failure nor defeat. Acceptance does not mean staying in situations that negatively impact your life when it is within your control to make decisions around them. However, sometimes life does present bigger hurdles than traffic jams, and we simply have no control over them; for example:

* Death
* Illness
* Loss
* Tragedies
* Other people's behavior
* Redundancy
* Relationship breakups

The most difficult arena in which I have witnessed the challenge of acceptance is in my work with the dying. After all, how can you tell a young person who is dying—perhaps leaving children, a spouse, family members behind—to accept their fate? Most people initially express a natural determination to fight. The journey has to be at their pace.

Yet, when every option is explored and treatment exhausted, sometimes fighting against the inevitable can make their distress worse. Refusing to move toward acceptance of any inevitable situation increases psychological distress and adds to the pain already present. The principle of moving towards acceptance helps ease the battle, reduce distress, and aid clarity, and ultimately it brings some degree of peace in the saddest of circumstances.

This is not giving up. This is not failure. It is embracing a path that was not planned or predicted and that cannot be controlled. It is following whatever the natural flow of life dictates at that time. It is staying present with what is and, within that, trusting that acceptance will, in time, bring peace.

Once I sat with a therapy client who had tragically lost her husband. She sobbed inconsolably, asking me why this had happened to her. I had no answer for her and could offer nothing more than my presence in that dark hour. In therapy a few months later, things were a bit calmer. She surprised me when she reported feeling sad but a little less distressed. I asked her why she thought that was and she said there were two key things:

- "I've stopped telling myself this shouldn't have happened to me, because it did, and I can't change that."

- "Despite the awful pain, if I continue to tell myself this is hopeless, then it continues to feel hopeless."

She was on her personal journey to acceptance. It didn't stop her sadness or grief, but it helped ease the distress that was adding to the pain that was already there.

## How This Links in to Ten to Zen

Each of us struggles with things we find difficult to accept. It would be wrong of me to adopt a forceful approach to this principle of acceptance, but I do encourage it as an option. Remember, this is not the same as saying that you shouldn't change difficult circumstances that you have the power and ability to change. It's about knowing what you have the power to change and what you don't.

I encourage you to accept that certain things cannot be changed and to just allow things to be. To accept what each moment brings, remember the following:

- What's happened in the past is over now; let it be.

- Whatever is to come in the future is not in your control; let it be.

- Whatever is going on now in your life, accept it as part of your experience and move towards it with curiosity; let it be.

So on the day you are feeling anxious, let it be. Try the principle of acceptance when managing your anxiety, move towards it and ask that part of you what it needs. On the day you are feeling sad or lonely, let it be. Try the principle of acceptance of your sadness, move toward it with kindness, and ask that part of you what it needs.

It is understandable that some view acceptance as a weakness or a sign of submission. In fact it is the opposite. It is the quiet, dignified principle of allowing things to be, trusting that as you move toward them with mindful presence, you will find a new awareness, new light, and more strength than you could have imagined possible.

## Accepting Yourself

Now it really gets interesting. How many of us can truly say we fully accept ourselves? As I've said throughout the book, most of us have aspects of ourselves that we find hard to accept. I hear them every day of my working life:

- "I don't like my body."

- "I wish I were more intelligent."

- "If only I were rich."

- "I wish I had made different choices."

I am sure most of us identify with these sentiments at some level. There seems to be an epidemic of dissatisfaction of wishing that we were different. Yet this dissatisfaction has a very detrimental impact on us. We listen daily to our self-rejection, self-disappointment, and at worst, self-loathing. Again, I want to stress that I advocate and encourage motivational, positive changes in life that will enhance aspects of yourself and your well-being. What I speak of here are those parts of ourselves that we sometimes reject but that *are a given*: our race, our sexuality, our stories, our families, our past, our imperfections, our personalities, the essence of who we are as people. The beautiful, rich tapestry of our humanity.

As I've said earlier, most people wouldn't dream of treating another person with the same level of harshness that they treat themselves. In its extreme, this becomes a form of self-abuse.

I have to acknowledge here I have some personal understanding of this area, which I feel is important to share. When I say we are all in this together, we really are. For me, my sexuality was a huge area of discontent and self-rejection for reasons I now understand. In my formative years, the general message for many gay people growing up in Ireland from some churches, areas of the media, and society was that it was wrong, sinful, and abnormal. I don't think there was ever any intention to hurt people, but fear does evoke strong responses. Of course, I was hugely confused growing up, as being attracted to the same sex was as normal for me as my brothers wanting to go on a date with a girlfriend.

However, I was getting a persistent message that these feelings were wrong and little reinforcement telling me they were OK, so I started to subconsciously reject this part of my self, hoping it would go away. In my mind, I was going to hell. No surprise, the feelings didn't go away and it was only when I came out and found the courage to accept that part of myself that I began to grow and gain some freedom. I remember someone saying to me at the time, "There are many different types of flowers in a garden, it's as simple as that." It didn't feel that simple at the time, but in reality it was.

## ⏱ Take a Moment . . .

Consider now what parts of yourself you find difficult to accept. I encourage you with a compassionate, open mind to try to understand why you reject these aspects of yourself. Make today the day you decide to stop the rejection. Each day, as you don your Ten to Zen "mental cloak," be mindful of the importance of accepting that which cannot be changed, the freedom of accepting oneself, the sense of peace that comes with accepting others.

## Accepting Others

It's a fact of life: some people are simply annoying. None of us can get on with everyone; it is simply not possible when we consider the vast ranges of experiences, personality types, cultures, values, and so on.

The reality is that that we often live, marry, become friends with, work, and co-exist with people whom we find, on occasion, difficult to accept. Then our brain's threat system can go into defense mode to fight off these others. We refuse to accept differences, and enter into a war of intolerance, maybe developing all sorts of theories about the other person:

- They don't respect me.

- They need to be taught a lesson.

- I hate it when they do that.

- They are deliberately setting out to upset me.

- I refuse to accept that.

Just as with the other aspects of acceptance, there will unquestionably be times when it is right and necessary to challenge unacceptable behaviors and make changes or get help; cases such as violence, bullying, humiliation, or abuse come to mind. However, there will equally be times when moving toward accepting the other as they are may lead to a newfound freedom and a healthier relationship with them.

Sometimes it helps to let the other person know how they make us feel, in the hope they can make some changes. But this may not always be possible and you may find greater ease in accepting the person as they are:

* The boss who never offers praise may not know how to do this.

* The partner who leaves the toilet lid raised may just not be as attentive as you.

* The friend who is always late is likely to be late with everyone.

* The child who doesn't do what they are told may have difficulty concentrating.

* The partner who finds it hard to be romantic may find it hard in general to express their emotions.

There is an expression I heard several years ago which has stayed with me when I think of how to deal with accepting others: *"Everyone's at fault but no one's to blame."*

Each of us on this planet comes with a backstory that can help explain our actions and behavior. My experience is that when people behave badly they often are doing so because they, too, are hurting in some way. When this behavior is damaging to us, we are of course justified in challenging this. But sometimes in trying to change other people's behavior, we just end up creating more distress and frustration for ourselves, and more resistance to change from the other.

🕐 **Take a Moment . . .**

The choice to be accepting of others is a highly personal one. I do, though, encourage you now to take a moment to consider those people in your life whose behavior you find difficult or challenging. Perhaps accepting them as they are might bring some peace for you.

Here are a few things to consider:

- Can you change them?

- Is this in your control?

- Is your battle with them helping the situation?

If you answered "no" to all three questions, then maybe it's time to consider allowing things to be and learning to start accepting the other people as they are, warts and all!

## Who's Pushing Your Buttons?

Another possibility to consider is whether the other person is setting off some of your triggers. These may have nothing to do with their behavior, but are actually more about how you perceive and react to their behavior. I think we can all confess to this at times. An example from a patient I worked with may help: "My boss never compliments me, which makes me think I'm not good enough. I decide to have an open, honest conversation with him. He tells me that he does value me and that he has been taught to behave in an aloof, non-complimentary manner because he learned from experiences as a child with his father that this would help him avoid being seen as weak."

Above all, always bear in mind that, like you and I, everyone comes with a story and a way of being. There are aspects of me that some might find difficult to accept; likewise with you. However, we are all worth accepting, despite our foibles and flaws; they are simply a part of us; they don't define us. *Every one of us is at fault; no one is to blame.*

Each day when you don your imaginary Ten to Zen "cloak," this becomes a time to consider how the principle of acceptance can enhance your life.

## Compassion

Sally was a client at one of my workshops who shared with me that she had experienced several years of depressive symptoms after her marriage ended and she was bullied at work.

She described many attempts at therapy, medication, and various programs that had no real impact. She then told me that she had decided to go off alone to walk the Camino de

Santiago route (a popular pilgrimage walk ending in northwest Spain). She met numerous people on her journey who made a significant impact on her, and she began to experience some peace and calm.

After a few weeks she reflected on all the people she had met who had influenced her and realized that they have two things in common:

- They took time out.

- They were compassionate to themselves and others.

Sally's journey toward finding her compassionate self had started. After spending most of her life blaming herself for all the adversities that had happened, she told me she was really refreshed by the Ten to Zen workshop, as it reflected her road to change. She was reminded of the importance of stopping, slowing down, regaining perspective, and living with principles of compassion, acceptance, and authenticity. I should add she joked that her pilgrimage walk was two months long. She hadn't realized that ten minutes a day could add so much value to her life!

## The Benefits of Compassion

We know from some of the great research in compassion-focused therapies that when we are operating from within threat mode, it is very hard for us to access our compassionate selves or manage our internal struggles. However, when we exercise compassion towards ourselves, the all-around improvements are astounding. Comparable research from

Buddhist and mindfulness studies tell similar stories. Most people look for ways to avoid, push away, or push down their difficulties. This is why comforts such as alcohol, drugs, shopping, sex, overcompensating, work addiction, and the many other strategies we all recognize become a means of managing difficult emotions. Of course, these all come with a price if they are not managed in moderation.

Compassion toward oneself simply isn't seen as an option for many people. It's often not taught or advocated in society as a sensible means of coping. I often hear people in my workshop express concerns such as:

- It's self-indulgent.

- It's not socially acceptable.

- It could be seen as weakness.

- I wouldn't know where to start.

- It's not the "manly" thing to do (for men, obviously).

I argue strongly that learning to be compassionate to oneself changes not only your world but that of those around you. It is not fluffy or selfish. It is only when we learn to treat ourselves with kindness and respect that our strength and internal power are fostered and our internal voice is no longer one of shame, judgment, and criticism but becomes kinder and more reasonable. Mistakes are OK. Perfection isn't necessary. Blame becomes a thing of the past. New possibilities and clearer thinking are endlessly available.

I delivered a Ten to Zen workshop to a group of plumbers recently. You can imagine some of the defensive banter that went on initially. I then made a simple statement and the whole mood changed: "If there is anyone in the room who wakes up feeling worthless more days that they would like to, or knows someone who is struggling in this way, then this could be a very useful day for you."

Suddenly their ears pricked up, their banter lessened, and I heard one of the clearest descriptions of what being compassionate to ourselves looks like. One of the guys in the group wanted to be sure he understood correctly and asked, "Are you saying that I simply need to look after myself when I'm struggling, like I would do with a best friend or my wife and kids?"

I answered a simple "Yes," to which he responded, "I get that, it makes sense."

And that's it, exactly. Looking after yourself in just the way you would someone you care deeply about. And I would extend this further to suggest that, as with the principle of acceptance, this compassion to oneself should also be extended to those around you.

 **Take a Moment . . .**

> Each day, when you put on your imaginary Ten to Zen cloak, bring to mind the second of the three principles, compassion. Then ask these simple questions:
>
> - How am I going to practice compassion to myself today?
>
> - How am I going to practice compassion to others today?

There is an expression that runs, "Kindness can change the world." Compassion starts with you. Living by this principle will start you on a whole new journey that can genuinely change your world and that of those around you.

## Authenticity

I started the book by asking you whether you are living the life you want to. Like most of us, I'm sure you have a list of things you would like more or less of. When I ask this question in workshops, the responses often evolve into fantasies about bigger homes, more money, less work, or life in a sunny climate. And it's great to have dreams. But I follow it up with another question that usually leads to nervous laughter, then a silent pause: "Do you think any of these things will truly lead to the life you want?"

The silence answers my question. I think we all secretly suspect that authentic living isn't really based on our successes, our wealth, or any other material gains we achieve. Experience has taught me that living authentically is an internal process. Whoever I work with, whether they are an A-list celebrity or a homeless person trying to get back on track, the one thing they share is their emotional struggles. These struggles don't discriminate on the basis of wealth or status. We are part of a shared humanity, and for me living authentically is living our humanity fully: joy and sorrow, strength and vulnerability, calm and chaos. It is standing on the stage of life, bearing whatever our truth may be with pride. I know this is not easy. Nothing worthwhile ever is.

Have you ever watched a movie or play and become so deeply moved by a performance that you almost believe the scene to be real? After seeing him in a play, I had the opportunity to chat with an actor who moved me in just such a way. I asked him how he could deliver such believable, raw pain on stage. He stated calmly that his technique was simple: "I tap into my own human pain; anything less won't translate as authentic, because I'm as broken as everyone else."

I was reminded then of the thousands of people I have sat with—both the living and the dying—as they bear their pain, and how much beauty there is in those moments. People who live authentically radiate an indescribable something that no product, lifestyle, title, or kudos can match. They are magnetic, because they are the people who are not hiding or pretending. They speak their truth. They can say "no." They can manage rejection. The number of likes or dislikes they get on social media has no meaning for them. Their sheer presence brings a sense of calm to others. They share their suffering and their joy equally. They present themselves authentically and their presence is contagious in the best possible way.

Each time I meet with such a person, I am reminded of the importance of the principle of authentic living. What is calmer living if it is not authentic living? I sometimes question whether we can have calmer lives if we are not living truthfully. At some core level we realize this, which creates distress. Living authentically is as necessary as the principles of compassion and acceptance, and has equal value. I have deliberately kept it as the final focus of your ten minutes, as I believe it underpins everything we are working on together.

## Authentic Living and You

I can offer no specific formula here as to what authentic living means for you, because each of our truths will vary. I do, though, encourage you to consider some of the following possibilities, as a means of honoring your authentic self:

- I will present myself as I am, and know that I am enough.

- I will make decisions that I know are good for me.

- I will be able to say "no" and make a stand for myself when I need to.

- I will commit to doing my best in what I do.

- I will allow myself to share both my darkness and light, with no judgement about them.

- I will take care of all aspects of myself, including my mind.

- I will stay present in the moment.

- I will observe when I am trying to please too much, overcompensate for something or gain approval.

- I will try to be the best, most truthful version of me, nothing more.

- I will appreciate and express gratitude whenever I can.

- I will remind myself that the only moment is now.

Each day when you put on your imaginary Ten to Zen "cloak" bring to mind the third principle—authenticity. Now, after having reflected on the above paragraphs:

 **Take a Moment . . .**

Take a minute to ask yourself, truthfully:
Can I commit to being my authentic self throughout my day?

## Finishing Your Ten to Zen Workout

You have now completed the final part of your Ten to Zen mind workout. I am confident that the principles of acceptance, compassion, and authenticity will enhance your daily workout, adding substance and depth to it. Beyond your daily workout, I hope these principles become integrated into your day as a constant reminder that you can live a calmer, fuller life. The donning of your imaginary cloak every day is a reminder of these principles, to support you throughout the day.

Here's a summary of the steps in your ten-minute workout:

| | |
|---|---|
| Minute 1: Step 1. | Stopping |
| Minute 1: Step 2. | Checking in |
| Minutes 2 and 3: Step 3. | Arriving in your calm space |
| Minutes 4 and 5: Step 4. | Breathing consciously |
| Minutes 6 and 7: Step 5. | Managing your thoughts |
| Minutes 8 and 9: Step 6. | Being in the present moment |
| Minute 10: Step 7. | Living with acceptance, compassion, and authenticity |

As you return to your day after your workout, I can promise that you will feel a greater sense of stillness, control, and perspective. In time you may want to take more Ten to Zen moments and some days you may need fewer. Ultimately, you will notice a difference in how you view life, and I suspect others will also notice a change in you. The possibilities ahead are endless. Using these ten minutes to create space between you and what goes on in your mind will allow you to achieve a new-found strength, power, and openness that may not have seemed possible before.

Although we have reached the end of the ten-minute workout, I am aware that there may be times when emergency situations call for something even quicker. Also, there are other lifestyle suggestions beyond Ten to Zen that may help you keep up the momentum of the work you are doing. So Chapter 10, your final chapter, looks at how to manage those emergency or crisis moments and contains a few suggestions for a Ten to Zen lifestyle outside of your daily workout.

# CHAPTER 10:

# Beyond Ten to Zen

Michael is the marketing director of a media company and approached me at the end of a workshop to say he was too busy to take ten minutes out every day. With a grin, he asked me if there was a quicker version. I, of course, advocate the importance of finding the ten minutes daily; however, the realist in me knows that sometimes life will get in the way. For those of you, like Michael, who worry about finding the time or that other things may get in the way, I'll explore these options here.

This chapter will also cover some of the practical issues that come up in relation to the workout and answer two questions that I'm often asked. I will also look at life beyond Ten to Zen, summarizing key lessons I've learned in my work. The benefits of my program don't need to end once you have completed your mind workout. These principles for living will start to merge into your day, and with a calmer mind you can make wiser decisions on how to live your life in a more adaptive and authentic manner.

# What If I Don't Have Ten Minutes but Need the Techniques in a Crisis?

This is one of the most frequently asked questions I encounter. People are often concerned that sometimes even a ten-minute commitment could be a struggle. As I have emphasized, most of us will commit ten minutes each day to showering or eating breakfast, and I stress again the importance of prioritizing your mental health. My experience is that, once people get into the rhythm of their daily Ten to Zen workout, they find it hard not to engage with it, as the benefits are so obvious.

That said, I am aware there will be days when you forget or the dog gets sick or the kids need help with a project or the builders are doing work in your home. I am also aware that difficult moments will arise when you need an urgent strategy. With that in mind I introduce you to your "Emergency Two to Zen." This is similar to your daily ten-minute workout but with one key difference—it is a two-minute workout. I repeat that it is in no way a *substitute* for your daily ten minutes. Remember that the research, particularly with mindfulness, informs us that the real changes occur with a certain amount of daily regular practice.

Here are some everyday scenarios I frequently hear as times when an emergency strategy would be useful. You may have your own particular triggers.

- A difficult meeting or interaction at work

- Public speaking

- A conflict situation, whether personal or professional

- An interview

- A date with someone new

- Having to break bad news to someone

- Managing a deadline or overwhelming pressure at work

- Studying for exams

- Coping after a breakup

- Bereavement

- Managing an unexpected situation

- Traveling

- Being required to make a tricky snap decision

- Difficulty coping with children or demands at home

## Your Emergency Two to Zen

Everyone will have different triggers. The important thing is to simply notice when your automatic responses have kicked in. Observe if you are experiencing any physical changes in your body, cluttered thinking, a raised emotional state, or difficulty focusing. When you have an emergency SOS moment, I encourage you to remember these crucial things:

- Whatever the situation, you are feeling overwhelmed because the threat center in your brain has been activated; it simply needs deactivating.

- Finding a way to stop for two minutes in a private space is the key to helping you do this. It can be a visit to the bathroom, a walk around the block—whatever is easiest in the moment. If you are in a situation where you can't leave, such as a meeting, then I suggest you go quiet for a few minutes. If anyone asks you to speak, simply ask for a few moments to gather your thoughts. Within those moments you deploy your emergency Two to Zen tools (see below); they won't know. I appreciate closing eyes in public may be more of a challenge, so keeping your eyes open is fine here.

 ## Take a Moment . . .

1. **Simply stop and check in**: What's going on for you? (approximately twenty seconds).

2. **Connect to your calm space**: Go immediately to your Zen-like, calm space using your visualization, your word, and ten bilateral taps (thirty seconds).

3. **Breathe**: Using three consecutive deep breaths, in for four, out for four (thirty seconds).

4. **Thoughts**: Notice which unhelpful patterns have emerged and let go of them immediately (twenty seconds).

5. **Be in the present moment**: Sit in stillness in the present moment, mindfully allowing yourself to be recharged (twenty seconds).

6. Your two minutes are now complete. Repeat to yourself, as you return to your situation, your principles for living: **I choose acceptance, compassion, and authenticity to manage this situation.**

This emergency Two to Zen technique can be used at any time and, if required, several times throughout the day. With regular ongoing practice of the ten-minute workout you will be less likely to need the emergency Two to Zen. However, it is empowering to know that, should you have moments of sudden difficulty or if unexpected events arise, you will have access to this "rescue remedy" at any point in your day.

# What Are Your Key Principles for Ten to Zen Living?

Much of what I offer here may seem like common sense, but when it comes to taking care of ourselves, common sense doesn't always prevail and reminders are often useful. The focus throughout the book has been on looking after our minds, and here are suggestions that will strengthen that commitment. These tips mirror those I suggest to anyone I am working in therapy with.

Think of it in the same way as you would a physical training program. What goes on at the gym during a training program usually comes with other suggestions that supplement your quest to change your body. These tips act as additional mental reinforcement for your mind, designed to supplement you through your day.

## Top Lifestyle Tips for Ten to Zen Living

### Know When to Ask for Help or Support

This is my first tip, as it's the one that most often gets neglected. Every one of us needs help or support at times. However, we often resist asking for it. We tell ourselves that we should be able to manage by ourselves, or we worry what others may think. In therapy and during workshops, I have lost count of the number of people who have uttered, "I wish I had done this sooner." We procrastinate, tell ourselves it will get better, and struggle on as normal until we become exhausted. If you need help—whether that is with coping at home, at work, or in life generally—seek that support. Most reasonable human beings respond favorably and empathically when we ask for support because they realize that it takes courage to acknowledge that you are struggling and they can relate to that. (If you are feeling very anxious or low and have concerns about how you are coping with your mental well-being, you may require more than what is on offer here. In that case I urge you to seek professional help. It is available. This work will support you, but there is no weakness or shame in requiring something more.)

Our minds, as we know, can become tired sometimes or a little unwell, just like our bodies. Asking for support or help when you need it is honoring your Ten to Zen principles of demonstrating compassion to yourself, accepting reality, and making an authentic choice that is in your best interest.

## Surround Yourself with Radiators, not Drains

There is an expression that there are two types of people in life—radiators and drains. Radiators pick us up and offer hope and support when needed. Drains do the opposite; they leave us feeling depleted. Sometimes it is worth considering the choices we make concerning our friends and sometimes even our family. It is not reasonable for another human being, whatever the context of their relationship to us, to drain away our energy or leave us feeling empty. It is certainly worth having conversations with such people, practicing compassion and trying to make changes, if they are able to take this on board. However, it may be necessary to let go of dysfunctional or toxic relationships. This can be painful but is sometimes essential for peaceful living. Surrounding yourself with people who enrich your life is honoring your Ten to Zen principles of compassion, acceptance, and authenticity.

## Take Responsibility for Your Life

This can be tough to hear sometimes. Each of us has valid, justifiable reasons for experiencing difficulties in our life. It's so much easier to get angry and blame the world, others, life for letting us down. It can momentarily feel empowering to stay in a victimized state because the problem ceases to be our responsibility; but longer term, it keeps us stuck. So here's the bad news: it is your problem. Now for the good news: you are the solution. Reading this book is a step toward taking responsibility for your own life, so I may be preaching to the converted here. My point is, all of what we need is already within us. Others can support us and help us, but ultimately the onus is on us to take responsibility for the life we live and make it the best one possible.

## Get Out and Do Stuff, Even When You're Not Feeling It

A lot of research has been conducted on what impacts our mood. When we withdraw, cease to engage in activities, and lose contact with people, changes occur in our brains which in turn impact the hormones that influence our mood. The simple act of getting out and doing something, whether it's a walk, going for a coffee, seeing a movie, or visiting a friend impacts our mood. In the world of cognitive behavioral therapy, this is known as behavioral activation. In scientific terms, the act of doing something helps enhance our serotonin uptake, which has a positive benefit on our mood and reduces anxiety.

## Exercise

Those with an aversion to the gym or any form of exercise may start to dislike me at this point. Relax. Doing a bit of exercise doesn't have to mean a rigorous training program or running a marathon. However, I strongly encourage you to engage in some form of exercise. Obviously this should be within your personal ability and without compromising your physical health. All the studies around exercise and mental well-being report similar findings: exercise improves your mood, motivation, sleep, concentration, and even your sex life. Apart from these undisputed health benefits, you are again supporting your serotonin uptake, which reduces the hormones that aggravate stress and increases your feel-good hormones. It's a win–win situation for mental well-being.

## Sleep Well

I think we all know the benefits of a decent night's sleep. Equally, we all know the horrors of lack of sleep. Reasonable, rational human beings can become demonic, and, yes, I am describing myself here. Again, the studies are all clear. Regular sleep improves our mental well-being, thought processing, and ability to manage our emotions. Sleep hygiene, as it's sometimes referred to, is an essential part of living well. If your sleep is particularly problematic, as it can be with mood and anxiety disorders, it may be worth considering professional help.

## Watch Your Diet

It's almost impossible to turn on the television without catching some program on the benefits of a healthy diet. As well as the obvious bonuses of managing our weight, such as looking healthier and feeling better, a healthy diet, or eating the "right" foods, is also important for the functioning of the brain. I am not a dietician or a nutritionist, but I encourage you to explore the benefits of foods that enhance mental performance and help maintain equilibrium. For example, numerous studies show that fish oils are helpful and excessive sugar exacerbates stress and can contribute to low mood. There is a mountain of material available on this online or in bookstores, but just a few small changes can make a significant difference.

## Take a Walk in the Park

There are few better ways of regaining perspective than walking in nature. We all get absorbed in our day-to-day issues and often can't see the forest for the trees. Find a place to walk that uplifts you in some way. Macabre though it may sound, I sometimes choose to walk through graveyards. Every tombstone there serves as a reminder of a life once lived in which the same trials and tribulations were no doubt experienced.

With this wider perspective, I am reminded that everything passes and nothing is permanent. As odd as it sounds, I find it liberating and comforting because in the surrounding of this final resting place there is an urgent reminder of the importance of living. As I said, I'm from an Irish family, and when my mom was alive she liked visiting graveyards with my dad, even when she knew she was dying; they would even bring a folding chair and sandwiches on summer days. At the time I found this a bit bizarre and got great mileage from teasing them about it. I asked my mom once what they enjoyed about sitting in a graveyard for a few hours. Her answer was simple—peace. I didn't understand at the time but I do now. When I visit her grave I am reminded there is only the now, and within that is to be found great peace. It provides freedom from the past and future. I would like to add I haven't yet gotten to the folding-chair-and-sandwiches stage.

## Allow Yourself to Be Human

This one isn't a favorite for any fellow perfectionists out there. We like to get it right and avoid mistakes. This can be a challenge for a huge section of the population. Being human at times can feel messy, which I'm sure we all know but most of us don't like to admit to. Yet in the mess there is great wisdom to be found. One of the things I enjoy most about my work is that, when I start to work with someone, I often hear despair gradually evolving into hope, which then resurrects to fully living. At the end of our work together, there are no promises that there won't be a fall in the future, but next time there will be more mental resilience and wisdom to manage the fall.

Allowing ourselves to be human means fully embracing it all: the difficult emotions, the failures, the disappointments, the mistakes, the regrets, the perceived imperfections, the temptations, the falling, and the getting up again. The getting up again will introduce new joy, excitement, hope, and optimism, and then we might fall again. In fact we will fall again, for that is the essence of our humanity. Many of us view our humanity as a weakness or failure, yet it is also a source of guidance and strength. In allowing ourselves to be human we strip away the rules and conditions that tell us that it's all got to feel good or we must be good all the time.

## Accept That It's Up to You

Earlier I talked about taking responsibility for your life. Now I am handing over to you the work we have done together. I predict that one of two things will happen:

One, after reading the book you will seriously consider some of what I have shared with you and make an effort to ensure Ten to Zen becomes a part of your day. You will opt in to prioritizing mental well-being, leading to really constructive, optimistic changes in your life. You will start changing how your brain works and how you relate to yourself; this workout cannot fail to make a difference if you commit to it.

Or two, after reading this book you will ponder some of the ideas, put the book away, and continue with your old patterns. Nothing changes.

*So which do you want? It really is up to you.*


I sincerely hope that you make a decision to opt in and that what you have read will inspire you towards the changes that may be necessary for living a calmer, more peaceful life.

Whatever is going on in your life at the moment, please know, above all, that there is always hope. If you are not feeling that hope at the moment, allow me to hold the hope for you, knowing that, in time, as you engage regularly with the Ten to Zen way, hope will emerge; it always does.

Just as the sun rises every day, so it is with hope. Sometimes we just need to stop to find it.

# Ten Final Lessons from my Work with the Dying

I started the book with stories from the dying, and that is how I am going to end it. Ten to Zen differs from many other meditation, mindfulness, and psychology programs in that lessons from the dying are a central component of my work. But I hope you have seen that this is not a gloomy, sad, or maudlin component—quite the opposite. These people often developed the gift of viewing life through a different lens. They were able to see beyond the darkness, and sometimes they offered me advice that was startlingly relevant.

However, I want to avoid creating an idealized picture that paints all dying patients as able to enter a state of new wisdom; that is not always the case. Some people remain angry or hold on to grievances, which in my experience can add to their suffering. As in living, in dying. The process of learning to let go leads to greater peace.

To end, here are the ten key lessons I learned from my work with the terminally ill:

1. **Nothing is permanent—so use your time wisely**. Try to live as if each moment, each day is a gift. Remember that whatever is going on in your life now will pass and there are lessons to learn from difficult experiences if you allow yourself to be open to them. Spend as much time as possible doing things you enjoy, and with the people you love. Plan the vacation, choose the adventure, prioritize time with family and friends.

2. **Learn to let go.** Let go of anger, resentment, grievances, revenge. In the end they will only cause you more pain. Freedom from these emotions is often found in letting them go.

3. **Take life less seriously.** Learn to have more fun, take more risks, and look for the joy in life that can be found everywhere.

4. **Keep it simple.** Try not to over-complicate things. We often clutter up our lives with complex situations, difficult relationships, or decisions that are not right for us.

5. **Live your truth.** Stay true to the values and principles that you honour.

6. **Leave a legacy.** Aim to leave something on the planet as a reminder of what you brought to your life.

7. **Don't tolerate bullshit.** I heard this so often that I had to include it!

8. **Aim for no regrets.** Try to live a life of "I did" or "I tried," rather than "I could have been" or "I didn't try."

9. **Suffering and joy are all part of living.** Accept them and let it all be.

10. **Live lovingly.** Reach out to those around us with kindness and love; in the end that's what really matters.

*Thank you for taking this Ten to Zen journey with me. It's been my privilege to share my experience with you. And remember, hope is possible in every moment.*

# Afterword

If you feel at any time that you need more support, please don't hesitate to ask for it. Ten to Zen is a life skill that I believe everyone can benefit from, but if you are still struggling, it's important not to be held back by a fear of labels or stigma. The statistics indicate that most of us will struggle with some aspect of mental health at a certain point in our lives, so there is no shame in acknowledging you may need professional guidance. Finding your calm and happy place is everything.

Essentially, the contents of this book are preventative measures to avoid things becoming more problematic than they need to be. If you are finding things difficult at present, what's in this book will ease your symptoms. However, if your mental well-being needs more support than I can offer here, I urge you to seek help from a GP, a therapist, or, at the very least, a friend. One of the biggest issues we have today is the reluctance to seek help. There is no shame or weakness in needing support. Likewise, if you know someone who needs help, pass on this book, encourage them to talk, provide them with information that directs them to help.

I have included details of some organizations that offer help and support, particularly in crisis situations. The organizations listed offer invaluable information and guidance, so I encourage you to explore what options may be useful for you.

Above all, I make a plea to all who read the book to talk, talk, talk about mental well-being. Talk about it in the bar, talk about it in the coffee shop, talk about it to your children, talk about it at work, talk about it with your friends. Spread the word. It's time to normalize this subject.

# Finding Help and Support

## Helplines, Websites, and Organizations

There are many organizations that provide support, including the following:

**For bullying:** www.stopbullying.gov

**For substance abuse and mental health support:** www.samhsa.gov

**For depression:** www.mentalhealthamerica.net/depression-support-and-advocacy

**For anxiety and depression:** www.adaa.org

**For suicidal thoughts:** www.suicidepreventionlifeline.org (or call 1-800-273-8255)

## Talk to Someone You Trust

If you don't want to speak to someone on a helpline, you could talk to a member of your family, a friend, or someone you trust, such as a teacher, your GP, a mental health or healthcare professional, or a minister or other faith leader.

Your GP or a healthcare professional can advise you about appropriate treatment if they think you have a mental health condition, such as depression or anxiety.

## Helping Children

If you are concerned your child may have mental health issues, then pay attention when they appear upset or withdrawn, encourage them to talk about their worries, and help them find their own solutions. You can also suggest your child talks to their GP or a counselor about how they feel.

## Further Information

You can find leaflets and information on mental health conditions—their causes, symptoms, and treatments available— through a number of reputable mental health organizations:

www.healthline.com/directory/topics

www.nami.org

www.mentalhealthamerica.net

www.mentalhealth.gov

# Acknowledgments

I would like to thank everyone involved in the journey of *Ten to Zen*. Special acknowledgments to my partner, Mark; my agent, Bev James; and my publisher, Carole Tonkinson—all who tirelessly believed in me and the message of the book.

www.tentozen.co.uk
@owenokaneten